...... Guide

Series editors: Ian Coffey (NT), Stephen Gaukroger (OT)
Old Testament editor: Stephen Dray
New Testament editor: Steve Motyer

Titles in this series

Discovering Genesis:
Crossway Bible Guide

Richard and Tricia Johnson

Crossway Books Leicester

CROSSWAY BOOKS
38 De Montfort Street, Leicester LE1 7GP, England

© Richard and Tricia Johnson 2001

First published 2001

British Library Cataloguing in Publication Data
A catalogue record for this book is available from the British Library.

ISBN 1–85684–202–9

Set in Garamond
Typeset in Great Britain
Printed and bound in Great Britain by Omnia Books Ltd, Glasgow

CONTENTS

Dedication

A number of people have helped us with this commentary. Ken and Jacki Turney and Alison Ives all read the manuscript at various stages and made useful suggestions; and Trudy Fejér drew the maps for us. Most of all, Lisa and Rachel, our young daughters, have ensured that the commentary would never completely take over our lives. Without them, it may have been completed more quickly, and we may have had more sleep – but life would have been a lot less fun! We therefore dedicate this commentary to them.

Seven routes through Genesis

The four main blocks of material in Genesis each make suitable chunks for studying in a series, but if you can only fit eight studies into a series here are some suggestions for cutting them down. (Of course, you may wish to choose others! Whichever you select, for the sake of continuity we would suggest the leader gives a quick résumé of the chapters left out.) We have also included several more 'thematic' routes.

Welcome!

These days, meeting together to study the Bible in groups appears to be a booming leisure-time activity in many parts of the world. In the United Kingdom alone, it is estimated that over one million people each week meet in home Bible-study groups.

This series has been designed to help such groups and, in particular, those who lead them. These Bible Guides are also very suitable for individual study, and may help hard-pressed preachers, teachers and students too (see 'How to use this Bible Guide').

We have therefore enlisted authors who are in the business of teaching the Bible to others and are doing it well. They have kept in their sights two clear aims:

1. To explain and apply the message of the Bible in non-technical language.
2. To encourage discussion, prayer and action on what the Bible teaches.

All of us engaged in the project believe that the Bible is the Word of God – given to us in order that people might discover him and his purposes for our lives. We believe that the sixty-six books which go to make up the Bible, although written by different people, in different places, at different times, through different circumstances, have a single unifying theme: that theme is Salvation. This means free forgiveness and the removal of all our guilt, it means the gift of eternal life, and it means the wholeness of purpose and joy which God has designed us to experience here and now, all of this being made possible through the Lord Jesus Christ.

How to use this Bible Guide

These guides have been prepared both for personal study and for the leaders and members of small groups. More information about group study follows on the next few pages.

You can use this book very profitably as a personal study guide. The short studies are ideal for daily reading: the first of the questions provided is usually aimed to help you with personal reflection (see 'How to tackle personal Bible study'). If you prefer to settle down to a longer period of study, you can use groups of three to five studies, and thus get a better overview of a longer Bible passage. In either case, using the Bible Guide will help you to be disciplined about regular study, a habit that countless Christians have found greatly beneficial. (See also 'Seven routes through Genesis' for methods of selecting studies if you do not intend to use them all.)

Yet a third use for these Bible Guides is as a quarry for ideas for the busy Bible teacher, providing outlines and application for those giving talks or sermons or teaching children. You will need more than this book can offer, of course, but the way the Bible text is broken down, comments offered and questions raised may well suggest directions to follow.

How to tackle personal Bible study

We have already suggested that you might use this book as a personal study guide. Now for some more detail.

One of the best methods of Bible study is to read the text through carefully several times, possibly using different versions or translations. Having reflected on the material, it is a good discipline to write down your own thoughts before doing anything else. At this stage it can be useful to consult another background book. See 'Resources' on page 14 and 'For further reading' on page 186. If you are using this book as your main study resource, then read through the relevant sections carefully, turning up the Bible references that are mentioned. The questions at the end of each chapter are specifically designed to help you to apply the passage to your own situation. You may find it helpful to write your answers to the questions in your notes.

It is a good habit to conclude with prayer, bringing before God the things you have learned.

If this kind of in-depth study is too demanding for you and you have only a short time at your disposal, read the Bible passage, read the comments in the Bible Guide, think round one of the questions and commit what you have learned to God in a brief prayer. This would take about fifteen minutes without rushing it.

How to tackle your group Bible study

1. Getting help

If you are new to leading groups, you will obviously want to get all the help you can from ministers and experienced friends. Books are also extremely helpful and we strongly recommend a book prepared by the editors of this series of Bible Guides: *Housegroups: The Leaders' Survival Guide,* edited by Ian Coffey and Stephen Gaukroger (Crossway Books, 1996). This book looks at the whole range of different types of group, asking what is the point of it all, what makes a good leader, how to tackle your meeting, how to help the members, how to study, pray, share and worship, and plenty of other pointers, tips and guidelines.

This book is a 'must' for all leaders of small groups. It is written by a team of people widely experienced in this area. It is available at your local Christian bookshop. If you have difficulty in obtaining a copy write to Crossway Books, Norton Street, Nottingham NG7 3HR, UK.

2. Planning a programme with your Bible Guide

This guide is a commentary on God's Word, written to help group members to get the most out of their studies. Although it is never ideal to chop up Scripture into small pieces, which its authors never intended, huge chunks are indigestible and we have tried to provide a diet of bite-sized mouthfuls.

The book is divided into four major parts, each with a title, indicated by a part-title page with a large number. If you want to get an overview of the Bible book in a series of meetings, you will need to select appropriate studies for each meeting. Read them yourself first and prepare a short summary of the studies you are tackling for your group. Ideally you could write it on a sheet of A5 paper and hand a copy to each member.

Then choose one study from the part you are dealing with as a basis for your meeting. Do not attempt to pack more than one study into one meeting, but choose the crucial one, the study which best crystallizes the message.

If you do not intend to cover the whole Bible book, choose a series of studies to suit the number of meetings you have available. Each part of the commentary is divided into a few (usually 10–12) studies. It is a good idea to use consecutive studies, not to dodge about. You will then build up a detailed picture of one section of Scripture. Alternatively, there are seven suggested routes through Genesis on page 9.

3. Resources

You will find any or all of these books of great value in providing background to your Bible knowledge. Put some of them on your Christmas list and build up your library.

New Bible Dictionary or *New Concise Bible Dictionary* (IVP)
New Bible Atlas (IVP)
New Bible Commentary (21st Century edition) (IVP)
Handbook of Life in Bible Times, John Thompson (IVP)
The Bible User's Manual (IVP)
The Lion Handbook to the Bible (Lion Publishing)
The Message of the Bible (Lion Publishing)
NIV Study Bible (Hodder & Stoughton)
The Bible with Pleasure, Stephen Motyer (Crossway Books)

The relevant volume in the IVP Tyndale Commentary series will give you reliable and detailed help with any knotty points you may encounter.

4. Preparing to lead

Reading, discussing with friends, studying, praying, reflecting on life ... preparation can be endless. But do not be daunted by that. If you wait to become the perfect leader you will never start at all. The really vital elements in preparation are:

▶ prayer (not only in words but an attitude of dependence on God: 'Lord, I can't manage this on my own')

▶ familiarity with the study passage (careful reading of the text, the Bible Guide study and any other resource books that throw light on it) and

▶ a clear idea of where you hope to get in the meeting (notes on your introduction, perhaps, recap what was covered at the last meeting, and what direction you hope the questions will take you in – don't force the group to give your answers).

Here is a short checklist for the busy group leader:

Have I prayed about the meeting?

Have I decided exactly what I want to achieve through the meeting?

Have I prepared the material?

Am I clear about the questions that will encourage positive group discussion?

Am I gently encouraging silent members?

Am I, again gently, quietening the chatterers?

Am I willing to admit ignorance?

Am I willing to listen to what the group says and to value their contributions?

Am I ready not to be dogmatic, not imposing my ideas on the group?

Have I planned how to involve the group members in discovering for themselves?

Have I developed several 'prayer points' that will help focus the group?

Are we applying Scripture to our experience of real life or only using it as a peg to hang our opinions on?

Are we finding resources for action and change or just having a nice talk?

Are we all enjoying the experience together?

What can we expect to learn from Genesis?

God's ultimate desire is to bless his creation within the context of a relationship with him.

God's people have a responsibility of stewardship over creation.

God reveals himself to people in very different ways.

God's desire is to bless others through his people.

God is always concerned for those least valued by society.

God chooses some very unlikely people to accomplish his purposes.

God especially loves those who, against all the odds, live their life believing that his promises will one day come to fruition.

God's greatest saints will face the greatest challenges to their faith – but even they are still human, and sometimes get it wrong.

God works on a far longer time-scale than us, and expects his people to develop patience.

God often allows sin to escalate – and then uses it to bring about his own purposes.

There is usually a sense of 'poetic justice' in the way God roots out sin from his people and from the world.

Reconciliation is close to the heart of God.

God remains with his people, even in the midst of the darkness.

Finding your way around this book

In our Bible Guides we have developed special symbols to make things easier to follow. Every study therefore has an opening section which is the passage in a nutshell.

The main section is the one that *makes sense of the passage.*

Questions

Every passage also has special questions for personal and group study after the main section. Some questions are addressed to us as individuals, some speak to us as members of our church or home group, while others concern us as members of God's people worldwide. The questions are deliberately designed

▶ to get people thinking about the passage

▶ to apply the text to 'real life' situations

▶ to encourage reflection, discussion and action!

As a group leader you may well discover additional questions that will have special relevance to your group, so look out for these and note them in your preparation time.

Stop and look

This feature gives us the chance to stand back from the action and take stock. It gives a summary of what to look for in the passages we are about to read, and useful background material.

Digging deeper

Some passages, however, require an extra amount of explanation. This spade feature indicates additional background material that helps us to understand something factual. For example, if we dig deeper into the Gospels it helps us to know who the Pharisees were, so that we can see more easily why they related to Jesus in the way they did.

The story begins

What kind of book is Genesis?

Genesis is a book of

> *stories*. Stories are designed to live within us, shaping and strengthening us by their kaleidoscope of patterns. They are there, like John's scroll, to be metaphorically 'eaten', and sometimes will be sweet within us, at other times sour (Revelation 10:9–10). They are not designed to be read in isolation, taken apart and reduced to a set of 'principles for living'. We should read them carefully and reflect upon them continually, asking, for example: Why has the author told us *this*, perhaps for the second time, but has remained silent about *that*? We should compare and contrast them with one another, for they frequently echo one another in the way they are told. Such echoes bind the stories together into a unit, so that the meaning of the whole becomes greater than the meaning of each part. We should enjoy the wordplay, the humour, the irony, rejoicing with those who rejoice, and weeping with those who weep. These stories are a gift from the living God to enrich our lives.

> *history*. It recounts the earth's creation, Israel's history, the history of the people of God – and, ultimately, our own history. At one moment it deals with the birth of the cosmos; at the next, the planting of a garden. God is concerned about the history of whole nations, but is even more concerned about Hagar, an African girl whose son is dying and who needs a drink of water. There are huge differences between our culture and that of the patriarchs, but the differences do not reach down into the depths of the human heart and our own history is not so different from theirs. We too are called to set out on a journey of faith, and we too make many mistakes. We too are capable of heroic gestures, and of messy sins. We too may be the object of his anger; but, much

more, we are always the object of his love. We too live in a world sculptured by grace.

▶ *theology*. It tells us about the character of God and his relationship to us. Remember that the stories *are* the theology – they do not simply clothe it. The stories speak of God, who speaks in and through the stories. At times, the patterns within the stories seem to be like the first draft for another, even bigger, story: the story of our reconciliation with God. For the God of Genesis is a faithful God, and the promises he speaks, the covenant he enacts, and the people through whom he works all find their ultimate home in Jesus, the one in whom his fullness dwells, who is truly his 'image', and who is reconciling all things to himself (Colossians 1:15–20).

▶ *proclamation*. When Genesis was written God's people were surrounded by various competing world-views and ideologies, and it was meant to counter them, to say, 'No! This is the way it was, and is, and will be.' And we, too, surrounded by even more competing ideologies, need to hear Genesis thundering against the distortions of reality that surround us, and which are also within us. We need to hear Genesis challenge our own prejudices and those of our culture, and indeed those of our churches.

Reading the story

As you read Genesis, think through the stories from the perspective of each of the characters involved, and ask yourself what was really going on within them. Think about how these stories resonate with those of your life, of your family, your church and wider community, and reflect on what God may be showing you through the lives of these men and women.

Remember that the characters are human beings. They are neither heroes – although occasionally they may rise to perform a heroic action – nor saints. Indeed, in many ways they are quite ordinary, with the same frustrations, doubts and failures as the rest of us. But this makes the message of the stories more real, for the God who touched their lives can touch our lives as well, and the God who shaped them and worked through them in spite of their failures, can do the same for us.

Genesis is honest about human life: deceit and drunkenness, incest and insensitivity, polygamy and family-destroying favouritism – all occur even in God's chosen household! Elsewhere there is a background of lust, hatred, murder and seduction; but also of unexpected goodness, wisdom, and people who have a relationship with God despite not being a part of his covenant nation. There are women whose cry for justice involves allowing men to use their bodies, and men whose fear threatens to tear apart their families. There are hunters, dreamers, shepherdesses, traders, empire-builders, priests, prime ministers and maidservants. There are mothers and fathers, sons and daughters. There are angels and animals, and a serpent. And then there is God: Yahweh, El-Shaddai, Elohim; the Most High, the Creator, the covenant-maker, the God of Abraham, Isaac and Jacob; the one who guides, tests and wrestles with his people; the one who draws near and whispers words of blessing; and the one who, at times, is far away. Genesis is a book about beginnings, but most of all it is a book about God.

We do not want simply to give answers in this commentary; instead, we want to make the text come alive, to raise questions, and to give, at times, new ways of looking at a passage. We want to get you thinking about the stories, to encourage you to think about how they might shape your own life and that of the world around you. We want you to let the stories live within you, illuminating your path as you continue your own pilgrimage through life.

Of course, we too have blind spots and prejudices – every commentator is profoundly aware of the things that could have been said over and above the things that have been said. It will be for you to take the process forward, to read more carefully and to reflect more deeply, so that the stories become ever more real and alive in your own life. We pray that the God of Abraham, Isaac, Jacob and Joseph; of Sarah, Rebekah, Leah and Rachel; of Hagar, Tamar, of the unnamed daughters of Lot, and of many others, may enrich your lives with his blessing as you seek to serve him better. May people who will never read Genesis for themselves look at your life and softly say to themselves, 'So that is what it means to walk with God!'

The structure of Genesis

The author of Genesis structured the book into twelve sections by using a formula the NIV usually translates as, 'This is the account of …' This may not be the best translation, however; it might be better, after 2:4, to say something like, 'This is the family history of …' These headings occur in 2:4; 5:1; 6:9; 10:1; 11:10; 11:27; 25:12; 25:19; 36:1; 36:9; and 37:2. They help to clarify the divisions within the text in places where the chapter divisions are not helpful. Thus we should note that Genesis 2:1–3 is integral to chapter 1; 6:1–8 is closely linked with 5:1–32; and so on.

The three biggest sections, which form the basis for our own division of Genesis, are

▶ 11:27 – 25:11 ('The family history of Terah', focusing on *Abraham and Sarah*)

▶ 25:19 – 35:29 ('The family history of Isaac', focusing on *Jacob*)

▶ 37:2 – 50:26 ('The family history of Jacob', focusing on *Joseph*).

Chiastic structures

Occasionally we have used a 'chiastic structure' to show the relationships between the stories. This was a common way of arranging a story throughout the ancient world, where stories would usually be heard rather than read. The story would build up towards a significant turning point, which would usually have a special emphasis, and then the second half of the narrative, while continuing the story, would reflect key themes or phrases in reverse order from the first half. This can happen at many levels, from a single verse to a whole book. The following short example from Isaiah 60:1–3 shows how such structures are usually written:

> A   Arise, shine,
> B   for your light has come,
> C   and the glory of the LORD
> D   rises upon you.
> E   See, darkness covers the earth,
> E'   and thick darkness is over the peoples,
> D'   but the LORD rises upon you
> C'   and his glory appears over you.
> B'   Nations will come to your light,
> A'   and kings to the brightness of your dawn.

When reading such passages look for what is significant about the turning point at the centre, and for the similarities and differences between the sections in each half of the narrative.

Who wrote the book?

Jewish tradition assumed that Moses was the author of Genesis (and indeed of the whole Torah, the first five books of the Bible). This tradition is reflected in the Authorized (King James) version, where Genesis is described as 'The First Book of Moses'.

Technically, however, the book is anonymous. No Hebrew manuscript of Genesis gives us an author, and if it was Moses, it is certain that parts have subsequently been edited (for example Genesis 14:14 [see also Deuteronomy 34:1] mentions 'Dan', which was not given that name until Judges 18:29, well after Moses' death). It is possible that the book came into being in gradual stages, from a number of different sources. (After all, other books such as Psalms or Proverbs were formed over hundreds of years, and indeed the Bible itself came into being in this way.) Those interested in this question might like to read the introduction to Wenham's commentary (see 'For further reading', page 186). Here we are trying to make sense of the text as it stands, where necessary referring simply to 'the author' or 'the narrator'.

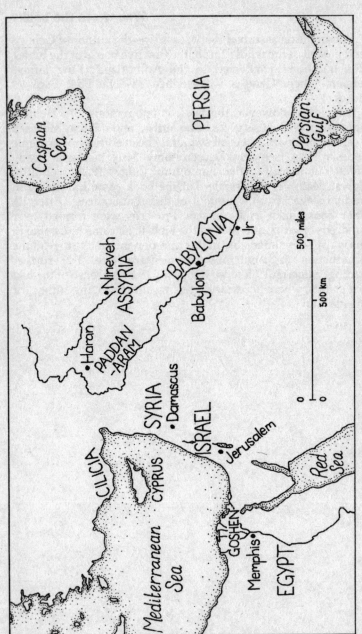

The Ancient Near East at the time of the Patriarchs

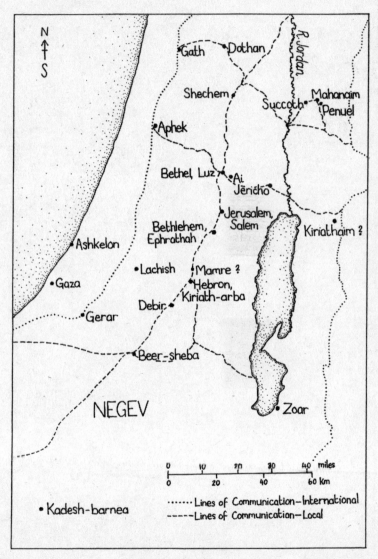

The Promised Land

BEGINNINGS

Genesis 1:1 – 11:9

Stop and look

These chapters describe how humanity is created in God's image, and placed within a world that is 'good'. But man and woman break their relationship with God, choosing instead to 'go it alone' into the darkness, nakedly facing death. God reaches out to them, and rumours of his grace continue to reverberate around the world. Although a few people choose to respond, the vast majority turn their back on him and insatiable pride and a lust for power become characteristics of human life. God's judgment falls on one generation as a warning of his ultimate judgment on all, but the generations that subsequently rise up are no different from those that went before. This, then, is the background to the dramatic way in which God seeks to re-establish a relationship with humanity, beginning with the man Abram.

The importance of the flood

The longest, and central, account in these chapters is that of the flood (chapters 6 – 9). It divides the whole section into two parts that parallel one another in the order and themes of their stories:

SECTION 1 (Genesis 1 – 7)   SECTION 2 (Genesis 8 – 11)

Creation (chapters 1–2) blessing on humanity (1:28)	Re-emergence of the earth (8:1ff.) blessing on humanity (9:1, 7)
The sin of Adam (chapter 3) Conflict between brothers (4:1–16) The curse on Cain (4:11ff.)	The sin of Noah (9:20ff.) Conflict between brothers (9:22ff.) The curse on Canaan (9:25ff.)
The 'ungodly' line and the development of culture (4:17–22) The pride of Lamech (4:23–24)	The nations and the development of empire (chapter 10) The pride of Babel (11:1–9)
The line from Adam to Noah (chapter 5)	The line from Shem to Abraham (11:10–26)
The call of Noah (6:9)	The call of Abraham (11:27ff.)
The flood (6:9ff.)	

Thus the flood makes no fundamental difference to human nature: afterwards events unfold in much the same way again. God's promise never to repeat the flood (9:11), however, prepares us to expect something different with the call of Abram; indeed, instead of curses and judgment comes blessing (12:2–3), first to the one, and then to the many (compare Romans 5:15).

Other themes

▶ The narrator often gives us the big picture, and then focuses on something more specific. Chapter 1 gives us a picture of the creation of the cosmos, while chapter 2 focuses on the creation of Adam. Chapters 4 and 10 give us a general picture of the state of humanity (the ungodly lines), whereas chapters 5 and 11 give details of the chosen lines who preserve 'the rumour of God'.

▶ Often a positive story is followed by a negative one. Thus the creation is followed by the fall, the chosen line (chapter 5) by violence and the flood (chapter 6), the covenant with Noah by his drunkenness (chapter 9), and the Table of Nations (chapter 10) by the Tower of Babel (chapter 11).

▶ These chapters have also been described by the expression 'spread-of-sin, spread-of-grace' (compare Romans 5:20): although humanity rebels against God and his punishment falls upon them with ever-increasing severity, his grace reaches out after them, mitigating that punishment and providing hope for the future.

Genesis 1 – 11 and Ancient Near Eastern mythology

Archaeologists have discovered tens of thousands of clay tablets in Mesopotamia dating from the first and second millennia BC. Some of these, which contain the *Enuma Elish*, the *Gilgamesh Epic* or the *Atrahasis Epic*, give us an outline of the religious beliefs that existed at the time, and include accounts of the creation of humanity and of the flood. The biblical writers were aware of these and at times mention certain details as a deliberate polemic or argument against the beliefs contained within these stories. For example in Mesopotamian mythology the gods were created out of Tiamat, who had the form of a sea monster. Genesis 1:21

states the reverse: it was God who created the 'great creatures of the sea'. Likewise the sun and moon were important in Mesopotamian astrology, but Genesis 1:14–15 'downgrades' them to being merely 'lights in the sky'.

Genesis 1 – 11 and science

Christians with a scientific background will need to wrestle with the relationship between their interpretation of these chapters and their scientific understanding concerning matters such as the age of the earth, the theory of evolution, the origin of humanity, the extent of the flood, the origin of languages, and so on. Numerous books have been written about these questions and in this commentary, because of the limitations on space, we have done little more than mention some of the issues in passing. There are, though, a few general points to bear in mind:

▶ Ultimately our understanding of God's world and God's Word ought to be in harmony (although no doubt there will always be fuzzy edges).

▶ Christians should not fear scientists, nor pay any attention to 'conspiracy theories' suggesting that all scientists have the hidden agenda of discrediting Christianity. This is simply untrue and is insulting to the many scientists who are themselves Christians.

▶ We all need to have the humility to accept that our understanding of the scientific data *or* of the biblical text may be faulty.

▶ We need to examine the different views with an open mind, being aware of the influences that have shaped our own understanding. We should also look at the best exponents of the different views, rather than those that content themselves with rubbishing (or worse, demonizing) their opponents.

▶ We need to recognize that for the biblical writer the scientific questions (the 'how?' questions) are secondary; the author is much more concerned with unpacking the character of God and his relationship to his creation, and especially humanity (the 'why?' questions).

▶ We all need to recognize that true Christians, with a genuine belief that the Bible is God's Word, have come to radically different conclusions about these questions, and we need to respect one another's beliefs and keep things in perspective. What we hold in common is *far* more important than the things about which we disagree. For example we can surely all join together with the heavenly beings in worshipping God as Creator (Revelation 4:11) whether we believe that the earth was created through the mechanism of the big bang 15,000 million years ago or instantaneously just a few thousand years BC.

It is not the purpose of this commentary to be contentious on these issues. Our concern is much broader, focusing on the issues we believe to be of greater significance for the majority of Christians.

Genesis 1 – 11 and the New Testament

As later Old Testament authors reflect on what God has done in history, they usually go back to the exodus, or perhaps to Abraham. In contrast the New Testament writers, with a reawakened concern for the purposes of God for the whole of humanity, often reflect the themes of Genesis 1 – 11. To mention just a few: Luke traces Jesus' genealogy back to Adam (Luke 3:23–38); the opening words of John's Gospel echo Genesis 1; Paul speaks of the role of Jesus in creation (Colossians 1:15–16), and identifies him as a 'second Adam' (1 Corinthians 15:45); Jesus himself, followed by Peter, comments on the story of the flood (Matthew 24:37–39; 1 Peter 3:20); and Revelation reintroduces the images of the serpent (Revelation 12:9) and the Tree of Life (Revelation 22:2).

Although our initial reading of Genesis must concentrate on the book as it stands, it is clear that a Christian reading of the book will, at times, rightly notice the reflections of these chapters in God's later revelation to his people.

Genesis 1:1 – 2:3

The creation of the world

Where does our world come from? What is the purpose of our life? The most fundamental of all questions begin to be answered in this chapter.

Genesis, the book of beginnings, naturally starts with an account of the relationship of God to the universe – his creation – and to the place of humanity within that creation.

God and his creation (1:1–25)

The universe we live in is not eternally old. It was brought into being by God (verse 1), who exists *prior to* and *outside* his creation – what we can see and touch is *not* the whole of reality. Nevertheless, as a painting reflects the character of the artist, so the world reflects something of God's glory (read Psalm 19, or Romans 1:20); it is of real value to him, for he has pronounced it 'good' (verses 4, 10, 12, 18, 21, 25, 31) and delights in it (compare Job 38 – 41).

In addition, God has created all the *processes* that exist within the natural world, and is actively at work through them no less than when he acts in so-called 'supernatural' ways. To believe that God *never* works in special ways lacks faith, but to demand that he should *always* do so is to lack maturity.

God, humanity and the world (1:26 – 2:3)

Human beings, created in God's 'image' (verse 26), have dignity and responsibility. They represent God in his world, and have the privilege, as responsible tenants, of sharing in his work, helping to make a world that reflects God's glory (verse 28). They also have the greater privilege of enjoying a relationship with God himself – of sharing in his 'Sabbath rest' (compare Hebrews 4). Indeed, the first full day of humanity's existence is a Sabbath (2:2–3). Both work and rest should be reflected in the weekly cycle of human life, but the time spent in God's presence 'ceasing, resting, embracing and feasting' (as Marva Dawn states in *Keeping the Sabbath Wholly* [Eerdmans, 1991]) ought to be the highlight!

Man and woman (1:27)

God loves and enjoys diversity. There are hints in the chapter of the community nature of heaven, if not of God himself ('Let *us* make man in *our* image', verse 26), and the creation is full of a staggering diversity of animals, birds and sea creatures (verses 20–25). Within humanity God has also created amazing diversity, of which the most fundamental distinction is between 'male' and 'female' (verse 27). No hierarchy is implied here; his commission to them (verses 28–30) is a joint one, and can only be fulfilled within the context of their relationship together.

Questions

1. What changes would bring your week more into line with the rhythm of work and rest in Genesis 1?
2. If God works in both natural and supernatural ways, how might you respond to a church (or an individual) that unhelpfully emphasized one at the expense of the other?
3. What do you think Genesis 1 might say to attitudes and ideologies such as racism, male chauvinism, materialism or New Age pantheism?

Understanding the 'days'

There are many ways of understanding the 'days' of Genesis 1. Three of the most common are as follows:

▶ The days represent *literal, 24-hour periods*. This has the advantage of being the most natural way many readers would understand the text, but it also presents difficulties: for example, in what form did light exist (day one) prior to the creation of the sun and the stars (day four)?

▶ Each day represents *a long period of time in the earth's history*. This has the advantage of giving due weight to the scientific understanding of the age of the universe, but has the difficulty of the order not matching the evolutionary sequence; for example, birds (day five) precede the land animals (day six).

▶ The author has described the creation of the world in *common human language*, which can be understood within many different cultures, and, inspired by the Holy Spirit, has structured his account in terms of a normal human working week. The earth begins 'formless and empty' (verse 2). The first three days (verses 3–13) give the earth form; and days four to six (verses 14–31) partially fill the emptiness, a task which needs to be continued by humanity (verse 28). The climax comes with the Sabbath on the seventh day (2:1–3).

In this view chronological considerations become irrelevant, as the author intended simply to write a thematic, theological reflection in which the two halves parallel each other:

without form ...	and empty ...
Day 1: light/darkness are separated	Day 4: sun, moon and stars created
Day 2: water and sky separated	Day 5: sea creatures and birds created
Day 3a: dry ground separated from seas	Day 6a: animals and humanity created
Day 3b: vegetation created	Day 6b: vegetation given for food
Day 7: Sabbath rest	

Whatever our view, we should remember:

▶ Genuine Christians have held all of these views (and several others). No view is heretical, and we should not insist that everyone hold the same view. The underlying theological principles remain the same for us all.

▶ The Bible uses language in all sorts of different ways. It is wrong to assume that literal language is more appropriate to God than symbolic, or figurative, language; indeed, judging by the example of Jesus, quite the reverse is true. Our understanding of the 'days' cannot be decided simply by an appeal to the 'literal' meaning; we need to decide instead whether the author *intended* his account to be understood literally or figuratively – which is easier said than done.

▶ The whole issue is complex, and there are many other arguments that have been used to support the different theories. It is important to read some of the more detailed literature before coming to a final judgment.

Genesis 2:4–25

The creation of humanity

Humanity has a special place within God's creation. We are called to live in a relationship with God and with others, and to be both 'carers' and 'namers' within our world.

 Genesis 1 has given us, truly, the big picture: an awesome, powerful God as the creator of the entire universe. This is balanced in chapter 2 by the picture of 'the LORD God' (note the more personal name) having a special concern for humanity, just a tiny part of that vast creation. Instead of a universe we have a garden; instead of the powerful words of creation we have God working as a craftsman, fashioning a man from the dust and a woman from the man.

The breath of God (2:4–7)

The world is not created so complete that nothing more needs to be done. Its future development will be a joint project between God and humanity (verse 5b). Throughout Scripture the development of God's kingdom is pictured as a co-operative venture between God and human beings. Paul comments later, 'I planted the seed, Apollos watered it, but God made it grow' (1 Corinthians 3:6). We should always be on guard against stressing one at the expense of the other.

In this context the Lord God fashions 'humanity' (the Hebrew word is *adam*) from the dust of the 'ground' (*adamah*). Thus humanity is well and truly rooted in the created world – but God's breath is also within us (verse 7)! We have 'the breath of life', we are 'a living being', and we can share in the life of God as well as in his purposes.

The garden (2:8–17)

As well as a craftsman, God is a gardener, providing a place of beauty for his people. The description of Eden is evocative, rather than precise: 'trees that were pleasing to the eye' (verse 9) allows each reader to picture them in their own way. Eden is a land of delightful trees, rivers and precious stones.

Where could such a garden have been? The mention of the Tigris and Euphrates (verse 14) has often led people to suggest somewhere in the Mesopotamian region; but the river Gihon (verse 13) may be the Nile. One helpful suggestion is that Eden represented the land of Israel itself, with the Jordan river poetically linking together the headwaters of the Tigris and Euphrates with the Nile and the Red Sea. Such an area represented the ideal borders of Israel in the Old Testament (Genesis 15:18).

Of course, no trace of the garden would remain after the flood. However, it would still be symbolically appropriate for God to give this land, and no other, to Abram and his descendants; and even more appropriate for Jesus to die on a 'tree' (1 Peter 2:24) outside Jerusalem to atone for Adam's sin of eating from a tree 'in the middle of the garden' (verse 9). In Revelation (21:1 – 22:5) 'Eden' and 'Jerusalem' are again merged in the description of the dwelling place of God, the 'New Jerusalem'.

In verse 15, Adam is given the commission to care for the garden. Human beings have the responsibility of stewardship in relation to the world around us. The destructive exploitation of the earth is an abuse of this commission, and a Christian worldview certainly includes a legitimate concern for the environment.

The helper (2:18–25)

God, who lives in the context of relationships, sees that it is not good for Adam to be alone. He begins by allowing Adam the responsibility of naming the animals (verses 19–20).

Whereas God is characterized by his power to create, he has delegated to humanity the power to name. Naming the world around us, and the things that happen to us, is a privilege we enjoy. We are all called upon to observe the world carefully and to name it truly, to clothe it in appropriate language, both the good and the evil. This provides a context for us to begin to think biblically and to live truly human lives. While naming what is good is the first step towards worshipping God, giving evil its true name is the first step towards its defeat.

As yet, for Adam, there is no evil, but there is loneliness (verse 20b). And to meet this need, 'woman' (Hebrew *ishah*) is sculpted out of the rib of 'man' (*ish*).

The woman is Adam's 'helper' (verse 20). This word (*ezer*) does not imply subordination; it is also used with reference to God himself when he intervenes in the life of his people (for example Exodus 18:4; Psalm 33:20). Gerald Janzen suggests the translation 'peer helper … Male and female are called to help one another' (*Abraham and all the Families of the Earth* [Handsel Press, 1993], page 42). Thus man and woman are equal, complementary, and incomplete without the other: both are needed to fulfil humanity's God-given commission.

Questions

1. How can we learn to give true names to the things around us and to the experiences we have endured?
2. How can your church put into practice God's original intention for man and woman, together, to fulfil his purposes in an equal and complementary way?
3. In what ways should Christians protest against the exploitation and destruction of God's creation?

Genesis 3:1–24

The beginnings of sin

Disobedience leads to broken relationships, and greater pain in our experience of life.

At the instigation of the tempter, Adam and Eve – already created in 'the image of God' (1:27) – seek instead to become 'like God' (verse 5), and the harmony depicted in chapter 2 is broken: sin, death and pain enter human experience.

The loss of innocence (3:1–7)

In the middle of Eden grow two trees, the tree of life and the tree of the knowledge of good and evil. Adam and Eve are forbidden to eat from the latter (2:16–17). The choice facing humanity, symbolized by these trees, concerns what sort of wisdom we choose to live by. On the one hand there is an *appropriate* wisdom rooted in a knowledge of God (Proverbs 1:7), which is described as 'a tree of life' in Proverbs 3:18. There is also a wisdom which belongs to God alone, 'too wonderful' for us to know (Job 42:3; Psalms 131:1; 139:6; Isaiah 55:8–9). If we strive to attain *this* wisdom, becoming 'like God, knowing good and evil' (verse 5), we are declaring that we are autonomous from God, refusing to live in a relationship of dependence upon him. Adam is warned that if he eats from that tree 'you will surely die' (2:17), that is, he would be cut off from God, the source of life itself.

The serpent approaches and tempts Eve. He casts doubt on the character of God (verse 5), deceiving Eve (compare 2 Corinthians 11:3; 1 Timothy 2:14) into believing that God's laws are for his benefit rather than theirs. She allows her eyes to be hypnotized by the beauty of the tree's fruit (verse 6), and assumes that God is denying her and Adam a 'good and desirable' experience which she feels they have a right to.

The woman – who has legalistically added the clause 'you

must not touch it' to God's command (verse 3; compare 2:17) – and the man both eat the fruit, and after they have eaten, their eyes *are* indeed opened. What they see, though, is their own nakedness, and what they know is shame (verse 7).

Passing the buck (3:8–20)

The garden is the place where God desires to meet with Adam and Eve, but instead it quickly becomes a place of hiding (verse 8). They recognize their nakedness, and are afraid (verse 10). Confronted with the fact of sin, Adam blames Eve, and implicitly God himself. After all, he says, 'you put [her] here with me' (verse 12). Eve then blames the serpent – 'It's not my fault' must surely be the oldest excuse of all!

Judgement falls on each in turn, and painful labour enters the experience of both man and woman. Their relationship with God and with the world around them is broken, and their relationship with one another becomes twisted. In this fragmenting world, domination rather than co-operation will henceforth characterize the relationship between the sexes (verse 16). Such verses, descriptions of the result of sin, are not God's ultimate purpose for humanity. It is always a part of the task of God's restored humanity, the church, to fight against the results of sin and to seek instead to be the kind of community God desires.

There is, however, a small ray of hope. One day the 'seed' of the woman will crush the serpent's head (verse 15), a promise which provides a goal for the genealogies that will follow later.

East of Eden (3:21–24)

God performs another gracious act in providing clothing for Adam and Eve (verse 21), but their life henceforth has to be lived 'east of Eden', away from God's presence. In this situation 'work' becomes 'toil' and, in the words of Ecclesiastes, 'everything is meaningless' (Ecclesiastes 1:2). Humanity's working of the soil (verse 23) becomes merely a reminder of creaturely status (verse 23; compare 2:7), and of their future destiny: 'dust you are, and to dust you will return' (verse 19). For human beings cannot now be allowed to 'live for ever' (verse 22): death, as well as pain, will characterize their experience.

Questions

1. How is your experience of temptation similar to, or different from, that of Adam?
2. How can your church better help its members in their personal battles against temptation?
3. In what ways should Christians be involved in taking the pain out of human experience?

Literal or symbolic?

God delights at times in communicating truth symbolically. Is this one of those occasions, or should we read the story literally? From a biblical perspective the answer to this question is probably 'Both.' Certainly it is crucial for Christian theology that there *was* a break in the relationship between God and humanity, as the purpose of Jesus' death and resurrection was to heal this rift.

In addition, it sharpens Paul's analysis of Jesus as the 'second Adam' (Romans 5:12–19; 1 Corinthians 15:22, 45–49) if the first Adam is a real individual. Thus Jesus, who reverses the flow of Adam's sin, is 'like God', but *refuses* to grasp 'equality with God'; instead, he chooses to be a servant (Philippians 2:6–8).

In contrast, the trees are given highly symbolic names, and some of the language about the serpent is also best understood in this way. It may well be that what we have is a symbolic description of what actually happened, using imagery that enables readers to enter into the world of the story and to understand better their own experience of temptation and failure.

Genesis 4:1–26

The spread of sin

Sin can never be restricted to just one area of life; its ripples spread wider and wider. So also God's grace flows into every area of our experience.

 Sin has damaged Adam and Eve's relationship with God and with each other. In this chapter sin spreads further: a family is torn apart and violence escalates (compare 6:11).

Cain and Abel (4:1–2a)

When Cain is born (verse 1) Eve may be hoping that he will be the one who will crush the serpent's head (3:15). In Genesis, however, any hope for the future *never* comes through the firstborn son – Cain will strike his brother's head, not the serpent's.

Names in the Bible are often significant. 'Cain' sounds like the Hebrew for 'brought forth' (verse 1); 'I have *gained* a man' gives a similar effect in English. Abel (verse 2) is the Hebrew word for 'breath', or 'vanity'; his life will indeed be as fleeting as the tinkling sound of a bell.

The murder of Abel (4:2b–16)

Both brothers bring an offering to the Lord; but Cain's is rejected, not because he offers 'fruits of the soil' (verse 3) rather than a blood sacrifice (in Leviticus 2 grain is a perfectly acceptable offering), but because his attitude is wrong. While Cain simply brings 'some of the fruits of the soil', Abel brings 'fat portions from some of the firstborn of his flock' – he offers the best he has (compare Hebrews 11:4).

Sin is like a wild animal 'crouching at the door' (verse 7) of Cain's heart, and Cain can choose whether or not to allow it in. Paul, reflecting on this passage, found that in his experience this same wild animal charged in at the first opportunity and,

41

he says, 'put me to death' (Romans 7:11). For Cain, though, there is still the opportunity to 'do what is right' (verse 7), but it is an opportunity he chooses to spurn. The volcano of violence in his heart erupts into murder (verse 8). Note how often the word 'brother' is used in verses 8–11 to emphasize the enormity of the crime.

After Adam's sin the Lord asks, 'Where are you?' After Cain's sin he asks, 'Where is your brother?' Again we have the denial of guilt (verse 9b; compare 3:12), the cursing of the ground (verses 11–12; compare 3:17), and banishment from the presence of God, 'east of Eden' (verse 16; compare 3:24). The sin of Cain thus reflects, and takes one stage further, the sin of Adam.

But we also have a sign of God's grace: as Adam was given a garment (3:21), so Cain is given a mark which forbids anyone from killing him (verse 15).

Lamech (4:17–24)

A short genealogy celebrating the gift of life to each new generation on earth ironically links Cain and Lamech, both murderers (verses 17–18).

Lamech wants to be 'like God' (3:5), having control over life and death. So he marries *two* women (verse 19), rather than one. He then kills a man in retaliation for an injury (verse 23), and boasts of his accomplishments in song (verses 23–24); but whereas God will only give sevenfold retribution (verse 15), he, Lamech, will be avenged seventy-seven times (verse 24). In contrast, God's people should do the opposite, and *forgive* others 'seventy-seven times' (Matthew 18:22).

But God's grace extends even into this family. Human culture and civilization develop, which compensates for the emptiness of life 'outside the garden'. Cain begins city-building (verse 17); Jabal, the life of a nomadic herdsman (verse 20); Jubal, musical entertainment (verse 21); and Tubal-Cain, industry (verse 22).

Cultural activities are not intrinsically wrong, for they can be used to glorify God. For example Abraham is a nomadic herdsman (Genesis 13:1–6); David, an accomplished musician (1 Samuel 16:18, 23); Bezalel and Oholiab, skilled craftsmen (Exodus 31:1–5); and the Lord himself makes a city, Jerusalem, 'his dwelling place' (Psalm 76:2; compare Psalm 48).

Nevertheless, it is easy to focus on God's gifts and ignore the giver. As Adam hid in the garden, so people can hide from God in a ceaseless round of activity that becomes an end in itself, rather than the means to a greater end. Perhaps these developments were placed within the line of Cain as a warning to us of their inherent dangers.

Seth (4:25–26)

With Abel dead, and Cain's line given over to violence, a new start is needed, a man through whom the knowledge of God can be passed on to succeeding generations. Thus Seth, through whom will come the chosen line of chapter 5, is born.

Questions

1. In what ways might we be guilty of concentrating so much on God's gifts that we neglect God himself?
2. What advice would your church give a young Christian who intends to make a career in the arts?
3. In what ways do you see people around you filling the emptiness in their lives that was designed to be filled by God?

Where did Cain find a wife?

The simple answer, within the framework of the Genesis story, is that Cain marries a sister, one of Adam and Eve's 'other sons and daughters' (5:4) whose names are not recorded. At this time there is no ethical or genetic reason for not permitting this. Much later, even Abraham marries a half-sister with no qualms of conscience (Genesis 20:12). The legislation forbidding such marriages is not given until Leviticus 18:9.

Notice that Seth, the 'replacement' for Abel, is born when Adam is 130 (5:3). Cain and Abel could easily have been born a century before this, and it is possible that, far from being two young men alone in the world, Cain and Abel were heads of their own clans. This explains why Cain feared retribution for his act (verse 14) and why he could so soon begin building a city (verse 17).

Genesis 5:1 – 6:8

'Generations come and generations go'

The passing of generations enables God's purposes in history to unfold, but it also allows wickedness to spread further on the earth. In our own generation, are we helping to establish God's kingdom – or to destroy it?

Many people find it fascinating to trace their family history. In this section we have the oldest genealogy of all: the line that links Adam, the first man, to Noah. It is a line that reappears in Jesus' genealogy (Luke 3:36–38);
indeed, it is a line that binds the human race together, as we are all 'sons and daughters of Noah'. It is also a line that shows God's purposes moving forward. History has a direction and a goal; it is not a meaningless cycle of existence.

From Adam to Noah (5:1–32)

Ten generations are listed, and their importance is shown by the amount of information given in each report. Three of these reports demand special attention:

▶ In verse 3 we are informed that Adam's son is 'in his own likeness, in his own image'. This echoes verse 1, and also 1:27, indicating that despite the introduction of sin, Adam's children still bear the image of God: there is still dignity and honour, as well as pain and shame, in human existence.

▶ In verse 24 we read of the mysterious 'death' of Enoch. Death is not to be feared for those who walk with God. A child once wrote, 'Enoch and God went for a walk. They talked for so long that at the end of the day, God said to Enoch, "It's a long way home for you. Why don't you come to my place?"' Death, for the Christian, is simply 'going home'.

▶ In verse 29 Lamech prophesies that his son Noah will bring 'comfort'. Unless intended ironically (humanity's labour ceases as the world is flooded), this seems to be a reference to the development of wine (9:20). Although drunkenness is consistently condemned in the Bible, wine itself is seen as a gift of God (for example Psalm 104:15).

Breaking the boundaries (6:1–8)

In contrast to the orderly progression of generations in chapter 5, these verses demonstrate the wider context of chaos enveloping the earth. The 'sons of God' have been understood variously as:

▶ *fallen angelic beings* (compare Job 1:6) lusting after human women. God's punishment (6:3, 7), however, is directed against the earth rather than the angelic realm;

▶ *descendants of Seth* (chapter 5) – God's chosen line – intermarrying with the descendants of Cain (chapter 4);

▶ *earthly rulers* (who describe themselves as 'sons of God' to bolster their authority) taking women they desire into their harem.

Whichever is the true interpretation, it is clear that the boundaries God has established for human life are breaking down. Wickedness has penetrated to the heart of humanity (verse 5), and God's heart is filled with the pain (verse 6). It is time for a new start.

Questions

1. Draw what you know of your own family tree. If you wish, add the generations from Adam to Noah at the top. Which figures would you seek to emulate in your own life?
2. 'The church is only ever one generation away from extinction.' What should we be teaching the next generation to prepare them to serve the future purposes of God?
3. If we took seriously that all human beings are related to one another, how would it affect our attitude towards events elsewhere in the world and in cultures different from our own?

How old was Methuselah?

The large ages given in chapter 5 have been a stumbling block to some readers. It is helpful to get an overall picture of the ages recorded between Adam and Moses (the ages in brackets are not given in the text, but are easily calculated from the information we are given):

Genesis 5		Genesis 11		Gen. 25:7; 35:28; 47:28; Exod. 6:16,18,20; Deut. 34:7	
Adam	930	Shem	(600)	Abraham	175
Seth	912	Arpachshad	(438)	Isaac	180
Enosh	905	Shelah	(433)	Jacob	147
Kenan	910	Eber	(464)	Levi	137
Mahalalel	895	Peleg	(239)	Kohath	133
Jared	962	Reu	(239)	Amran	137
Enoch	365	Serug	(230)	Moses	120
Methuselah	969	Nahor	(148)		
Lamech	777	Terah	205		
Noah	950				

There are two main interpretations of these ages.

1. The figures are intended *literally*. Arguments in favour of this include the following:

▸ Many cultures have traditions of longevity for their ancestors;

▸ human beings would naturally live longer when first created; the decline set in only after the flood, when life-spans reduced to 120 years (prophesied in 6:3) at the time of Moses.

2. The figures are intended *symbolically*. For example, the number seven, symbolizing for the author completeness or perfection, frequently appears:

▶ the ages in Genesis 5 add up to 8,575 (= 25 × 7 × 7 × 7)

▶ the seven ages in the third column add up to 1,029
(= 3 × 7 × 7 × 7)

▶ the ages of all twenty-six generations add up to 12,600
(= 70 × 180)

The *first* and *third* columns have much in common. Unlike the figures in the *middle* column, the ages at death are given to us; and each column begins and ends with a character with whom God makes a significant covenant. If we look at these two columns together, we notice that

▶ the seventeen ages add up to 9,604 (= 4 × 7 × 7 × 7 × 7)

▶ the middle age is that of Lamech (777)

▶ the seven ages on either side of Lamech add up to 7,777

The recurrence of the number seven would indicate that the period between Adam and Moses was seen as 'complete'. More importantly, it suggests that the birth and death of individuals, whether their life is long or short, are not random events. Their true significance, however, can only be seen in the light of a bigger pattern. Individuals are incomplete in themselves, but together God's people can reveal something of his perfect character (compare Revelation 7:4).

However we may choose to interpret the ages, it is worth recalling that

▶ although the ages seem large to us, the original readers would have thought of them as being small. For example, in the list of Babylonian kings, Alulim, the first king, reigned 28,800 years;

▶ *none* of the ages reaches 1,000, which in the ancient world would have symbolized some degree of divinity;

▶ *none* of the characters achieves immortality on earth (as again occurs in the legends of the cultures surrounding Israel). As Paul says, 'death reigned from the time of Adam to the time of Moses' (Romans 5:14).

Genesis 6:9 – 7:24

The world washed clean

God demonstrates great patience towards those who rebel against him, but ultimately sin will be destroyed, and there will be a cleansing of God's creation.

In chapter 5 there are 1,656 years from the creation of Adam to the flood. During this period sin has spread, affecting individuals, families, whole societies and ultimately the whole world (6:11–12). God has commanded  humanity to 'be fruitful' and to 'fill the earth' (1:28), but now Nephilim are being brought forth (verse 4) and violence is filling the earth (verse 11; compare 4:23–24). Barriers are breaking down (6:1–8), and the time has come for judgment, a judgment in which more barriers will be broken – those between land and sea, and sea and sky (1:6–10). However, a select group of people and animals will be chosen to repopulate a cleansed earth.

Note how carefully structured the story is between the two parts of Noah's genealogical report:

A	After Noah is 500 years old, he fathers Shem, Ham and Japheth	5:32
B	The sins of the sons of God, and of humanity	6:1–8
C	The corruption of the earth and the covenant with Noah	6:9–22
D	Entering the ark in Noah's 600th year; they wait seven days	7:1–16
E	For forty days the waters come upon the earth	7:17
F	Waters cover the mountains for 150 days	7:18–24
G	'But God remembered Noah'	8:1a
F'	Waters recede for 150 days; mountains appear	8:1b–5
E'	After forty days the raven is released	8:6–7
D'	Seven days' mentioned; they leave the ark in Noah's 601st year	8:8–19
C'	Establishing the covenant with Noah	8:20 – 9:17
B'	The sins of Noah, and of his son	9:18–27
A'	After the flood Noah lived 350 years.	9:28–29

Altogether, Noah lived 950 years, and then he died.

Noah's righteousness and obedience (6:9 – 7:5)

In the midst of a violent, corrupt people Noah stands out as 'righteous', 'blameless', and 'walking with God' (verse 9; compare 7:1). Similarly Paul writes that we should be 'children of God without fault in a crooked and depraved generation, in which you shine like stars in the universe ...' (Philippians 2:15).

It is difficult to imagine what Noah must feel when God tells him to build a vessel '450 feet long' (verse 15), and to populate it with animals. We *are* told of his obedience, however, and for this he receives a place among the heroes of faith in Hebrews 11 (verse 7).

Noah has to take two of each unclean animal, but seven of each 'clean' animal (verse 2) (a distinction later put into writing in Leviticus 11). The old man, in a covenant relationship with God (6:18), is here a model of the obedience later expected of a 'righteous' Israelite.

Entering the ark (7:6–16)

Noah, his family and the animals enter the ark (verses 7–9; 13–16), and at the right moment the Lord shuts the door (verse 16). Forty days and nights of rain follow (verses 10–12).

Waters cover the earth (7:17–24)

The rhythm and repetitions of verses 17–23 produce a sombre effect. Listen to the waves of language rolling in as the waters rise (verses 17, 18, 19, 20), and the quietness left as 'every living thing' (verses 21, 22, 23), the work of God's creation (1:20–31), perishes. Then 150 days pass (verse 24).

Questions

1. How can we test whether unusual commands are from God or not?
2. How can your church seek to live 'blameless among the people' (verse 9)?
3. God is so concerned for the individual species he has created that he saves them from the flood. How can Christians reflect this aspect of God's character in relation to the conservation movement?

Did the flood cover the whole earth?

Christians have disagreed for many years on the extent of the flood. The two main possibilities are that it was (1) *global*, covering the entire planet; (2) *continental*, covering the entire Ancient Near East.

At first sight a global flood seems to fit the language of the story better, but we need to be careful. Note that the Hebrew word for 'earth' (*eretz*) can also mean 'land'. The same word is used in Genesis 41:56, where the NIV translates it 'country'. The word 'all' should be interpreted in the context of the perspective of the observer, or writer. For example 1 Kings 18:10 does not imply that Ahab searched for Elijah in Latin America (compare Deuteronomy 2:25; Colossians 1:23)!

If you imagine the flood story being told by someone on the ark and substitute 'land' for 'earth' you get a different perspective. Ultimately, though, the extent of the flood is secondary to what God intends to communicate through the story, and this remains true irrespective of how deep the water was. As Christians, one of our main duties is to keep a sense of perspective about such issues.

Genesis 8:1–22

A new start

God develops our faith (and usually our patience!) by placing us in situations where we have to depend on him completely.

The narrator does not try to tell us what was going through Noah's mind and heart during this period, a devastation unique in the world's history. His silence is more eloquent than words. But now Noah and his family are

in a situation completely out of their control, with no idea of how long it might last. His faith was tested in the building of the ark; now it is tested again as he waits for God to act, and to bring him to a place of safety.

God remembers Noah (8:1–5)

Often a short phrase can be a significant turning point in a story. 'God remembered Noah' (verse 1) is such a phrase. To 'remember' does not mean that he has forgotten them, but for God 'to remember' is to *act* on behalf of someone. Later in Genesis God 'remembered Rachel' (30:22), and she bears a son; in Exodus 2:24 he 'remembered his covenant with Abraham', and begins to deliver his people from Egypt; in 1 Samuel 1:19 he 'remembered' Hannah, and she also bears a son. Thus he 'remembered Noah', and sends a wind, and the waters begin to recede.

It is a good biblical prayer for God to remember us. 'According to your love remember me', says the psalmist (25:7); and as a community Israel sing, 'Remember the people you purchased of old' (Psalm 74:2). Lord, remember us; we need you to act on our behalf!

But *we* must also remember something: God usually works more slowly than we would wish. As the Lord and not the slave of time, he takes his time, and does things at the right time (Romans 5:6; Galatians 4:4). For 150 days (verse 3) Noah sees no evidence that the water is receding, and then, at last, they feel the ark touch solid rock (verse 4). Another 74 days pass before they see the mountain tops (verse 5).

Testing the waters (8:6–14)

When God first created the earth, 'darkness was over the surface of the deep, and the Spirit of God was hovering over the waters' (Genesis 1:2). The flood brings the earth back to its starting point, reversing the distinctions made in Genesis 1. The waters again cover the earth, and, echoing 1:2, a wind from God blows over their surface (verse 1), and a raven, released by Noah, flies back and forth, watching for the land to reappear (verse 7). Just as there was a time of creation, and of 'uncreation', so there will also be a time of 're-creation' – resurrection always follows death.

The waters are, indeed, drying up, and to test the extent of this Noah sends out a dove at weekly intervals. Even when God himself is at work, we are not called to be passive bystanders; it is never unspiritual to assess what is happening around us. 'Test everything', Paul commands the Thessalonians (1 Thessalonians 5:21).

Three months after the mountains become visible, the water is gone (verse 13). Eight weeks later, the earth is 'completely dry' (verse 14).

A new start and a new promise (8:15–22)

Noah's family and the living creatures emerge from the ark, and are once more given the charge to 'be fruitful and increase in number' (verse 17; compare 1:22). Noah expresses his public thanksgiving to God in a sacrifice (verse 20).

Ordinary human language is used to describe the Lord's response: 'smelling' the aroma (verse 21) is a way of saying that he accepts Noah's offering. In addition, he decides that what he has done once he will not do again. Human beings have died, but human nature remains much the same (verse 21; compare 6:5). God promises not to destroy the living creatures (verse 21), and he promises humanity an orderly sequence of seasons, a framework in which they can live and work (verse 22). This would be especially important to the Israelites, surrounded as they were by cultures who feared that spring or harvest will not return, and who needed elaborate fertility rites to encourage the gods to extend the earth's history for another year.

God promises that he will not destroy all living creatures (verse 21), but he does not guarantee to prevent the human race from doing so, either slowly, through the destruction of the environment, or quickly, through the abuse of nuclear power. Humanity has the technology to destroy 'all living creatures', to damage the world's ecosystems irreversibly, or to create a nuclear winter that will not be followed by another spring. And God, as the sovereign Lord of history, does not guarantee to prevent this, should we choose to walk down that road. Indeed, he may even allow it if it is the only way to encourage people to repent (compare Revelation 8:6–12). The only guarantee we have is that in the midst of such destruction, 'one like a son of man' will be standing alongside us (Revelation 1:13; Matthew 28:20; compare Daniel 3:25).

Questions

1. What situations are there in your own life in which you might pray for God to 'remember' you?
2. What measure might your church use to test, or evaluate, what God is doing among you?
3. How might Christians act to prevent humanity doing what God has promised not to do: to destroy all life on earth?

Genesis 9:1–29

The rainbow covenant

God's words provide us with a framework for human life, and remind us that he is committed to his people, but we must always beware of sin, 'the enemy within'.

 The flood is over, but there is still unfinished business. God has promised to establish his covenant with Noah (6:18), and this he now does, recommissioning humanity in its task and committing himself not to send another flood. Despite everything that has happened, however, sin is still present within the human heart.

Recommissioning humanity (9:1–7)

This section is a restatement of God's original commands to humanity in 1:28–30. There is still blessing, and the command to be fruitful begins and ends the speech (verses 1, 7), but other aspects have become marred. Instead of humanity's benevolent 'rule' over creation (1:28), creatures will go in fear of people (9:2), and the animal kingdom is now, perhaps pragmatically, added to the human diet (verse 3).

Life, nevertheless, remains sacred. Our fellow human beings are still made in God's image (verse 6) and murder is thus a particularly grievous offence (verses 5–6). But 'murder' may be too safe and too distant an interpretation of verse 5; will not God 'demand an accounting' from us, if by our *inaction* we have allowed people to die, or to live blighted lives, when we *could* have made a difference?

God hangs up his bow (9:8–17)

God now makes explicit his commitment not to destroy the world with another flood (verses 8–11). Perhaps recognizing that Noah needs greater reassurance, he specifies that the rainbow will be a sign of this covenant (verses 12–17) – he has, as it were, hung up his bow in the sky, so that it no longer points towards the earth (compare Habakkuk 3:9).

We are told little in the Bible about God's relationship to the animal kingdom. He is, of course, their creator (1:20–25), and in this passage his covenant is not just with humanity but with 'every living creature' on earth (verses 10, 15, 16, 17). In addition, God will 'demand an accounting' from every animal (verse 5). In its teaching the church has often been in danger of ignoring or sentimentalizing animals but they clearly play a role in God's purposes. We should respect them as a part of his creation, and we are accountable to God for our stewardship of them. How we treat a painting says something about how we view the artist.

The cursing of Canaan (9:18–29)

In this section there are many echoes of the events of Genesis 3 – 4. Once again fruit provides the opportunity for sin, followed by the discovery of nakedness, and the provision of a covering. Again, there is conflict between brothers and, whereas earlier there was a curse on 'Cain' (4:11), now there is a curse on 'Canaan' (verse 25). These allusions to the earlier stories are meant to show that the sin which characterized human existence before the flood is going to continue in much the same way. There is still evil at the heart of humanity (8:21). Water may have washed the earth clean, but it will require a different washing to deal with the root of the problem (compare John 13:8; 1 Corinthians 6:11).

The disrespect shown by Noah's youngest son, Ham, leads to the cursing of Canaan, Ham's youngest son (10:6). In a society that places great importance on family relationships it is accepted that if the head of a family sins, the whole family bears the punishment (compare Achan's family in Joshua 7:24). As a basic principle, this ought to be a great motivation to avoid sin; it is, after all, sobering to think that others might suffer if *I* sin. However, it can (and does) lead to accusations of unfairness: 'The fathers have eaten sour grapes, and the children's teeth are set on edge' becomes a proverb in Israel (Jeremiah 31:29; Ezekiel 18:2).

This is still true as a basic feature of human life: the innocent suffer because of the sins of the guilty, who are often those in authority over them. But it will not be forever true. After quoting the proverb above, Jeremiah continues, 'days are coming ... when ... whoever eats sour grapes – his own teeth will be set on edge' (31:27, 30); and Ezekiel says, 'you will no longer quote this proverb in Israel'. Instead, 'The soul who sins is the one who will die' (18:3–4).

Questions

1. In the light of 1:29 and 9:3, do you think that Christians should support or oppose a vegetarian lifestyle. Why?
2. How can the church respond to accusations that God is unjust in allowing the innocent to suffer because of the sins of those who have power over them?
3. We are held accountable for 'the life of our fellow man' (verse 5). What should our priorities be when we are bombarded by information about needy situations around the world?

Genesis 10:1 – 11:9

The spread of the nations

Humanity will inevitably fulfil God's ultimate purposes; it may do so voluntarily, under his blessing, or against its will, under his judgment.

In this section the spread of the nations is depicted in both a positive and a negative light. In chapter 10, Noah's descendants spread across the world, forming different nations with their own languages, apparently under God's blessing (9:1, 7). In chapter 11 the dispersal and the division into languages is a judgment upon the pride of humanity. Such ambiguity is characteristic of the way the biblical authors depict many cultural activities, which can either truly glorify God, or be used to hide from him (see notes on 4:17–24, page 42). A nation, or an empire, can be a servant of God (as in Romans 13:4), but it can easily slip into becoming his opponent (as in Revelation 13).

In the list in Genesis 10 there are precisely seventy names, which indicates a sense of completeness, although the list is not intended to be exhaustive. Some of the names are clearly personal names, others are the names of people groups, or places. The nations are categorized according to racial, geographical, linguistic and occupational factors – note that 'son of' may, in places, refer to political allegiances rather than a biological connection.

The Japhethites (10:1–5)

As usual, the author lists first those genealogical lines less significant for his overall purpose. The Japhethites are primarily sea-faring peoples, located to the north of Israel, with whom Israel has least contact during her history.

The Hamites (10:6–20)

Some of these names, such as Cush, are clearly linked with north-east Africa, but there is no evidence that the author equated the Hamitic peoples with the Negroid races. Indeed, all the evidence points in the other direction. The most basic shared characteristic of these peoples is their preference for city-building, and the fact that they are later enemies of Israel. Thus the three most significant regions described in this section are

▶ *Canaan* (verses 15–19), which is full of city-states when Israel later conquers the land (compare Joshua 12:7–24);

▶ *Mesopotamia* (verses 8–12), which in secular history has traditionally been regarded as 'the cradle of civilization' where the first urban centres arise. Nineveh and Babylon, both of which were powerful enemies of Israel in later years, are each placed here.

▶ *Philistia* (verse 14). The five cities of the Philistines are a constant threat during much of Israel's later history.

The Semites (10:21–32)

The Semites are depicted as dwellers in the hill country, and are that branch of the family tree through which Israel comes. It is possible that the name 'Hebrew' comes from 'Eber' (verses 24–25), although this cannot be proven. The 'division of the earth' in the time of Peleg (verse 25) may well be a reference to the following story.

Babel's rebels begin babbling (11:1–9)

In the Bible Babylon is the archetypal enemy of God, striving to reach heaven and become like God. In 10:8 'Nimrod', the founder of Babylon, has the meaning 'we shall rebel'. Isaiah later taunts the king of Babylon with wanting to reach heaven and become 'like the Most High' (Isaiah 14:12–15), but instead he is cast down to the earth. Daniel 4 depicts Nebuchadnezzar, king of Babylon, as being like a tree whose top touches the sky – but is then cut down. Babylon rises again, only to be thrown down, in Revelation 17 – 18.

The story of 'the Tower of Babel' (Babel = Babylon), like the passages mentioned above, attacks the pretensions of Babylonian ideology, and by extension any community that models itself on Babylon's pattern. It is full of wordplay and irony in the original Hebrew. They want to build a skyscraper, but fall so far short that God has to 'come down' to see it! They don't even use stone, but Mesopotamian bricks. They seek a name for themselves, but instead their language is confused. They refuse to spread over the earth under God's blessing (compare chapter 10), but are forced to do so under his judgment.

The sin of the Babylonians is their desire to be 'like God'. In their pride they repeat Adam's sin and walk in Cain's footsteps, travelling to the east (verse 2) where they build a city (verse 4; compare 4:16–17). They seek to build a tower as a unifying focus for their community, to fill the 'God-shaped void' in their lives. How often have nations embarked on impressive building projects for precisely that reason!

When God created humanity he used the plural form ('Let *us* make man', 1:26) as a reminder to us of the need for community. The plural form is again used here ('let *us* go down', verse 7) because this human community has become so proud that it embarks on the project of seeking autonomy from God's community. Evil has to be restrained, and humanity must be dispersed into many smaller groups, each speaking its own language.

In Acts 2 the day of Pentecost is the theological reversal of Babel. Again, a group of people speaking one language are gathered together; the Spirit comes down upon them and they begin to speak different languages. But the purpose is very different! Rather than resulting in confusion, the profusion of languages leads to communication with people from throughout the 'Table of Nations' listed in Acts 2:9–11. Thus begins the process of reunifying people from every nation into one people of God.

God desires that the church, too, should 'be fruitful and increase in number and fill the earth' (9:1). Whenever it seeks to 'make a name for itself', building ecclesiastical 'cities' and 'towers' (verse 4), and hoping that they will reach up to heaven, it is modelling itself on Babel and denying its true vocation.

Questions

1. In what ways is it right to seek to be 'like God', and in what ways is it a sin?
2. In what ways do you think the church is in danger of repeating the sin of Babel?
3. What projects does your nation aspire to, which are intended by the government to glorify the state rather than God?

2

THE STORY OF ABRAHAM

Genesis 11:10 – 24:67

Stop and look

The rest of the book of Genesis revolves around one family, or clan – that of Terah. Like Adam, Terah has three named sons, one of whom dies early, and one of whom (Abram, later called Abraham) is chosen by God to continue the chosen line. In order to make sense of the stories it is helpful to get an overview of the whole family tree, as outlined in Genesis 11:27 – 35:29:

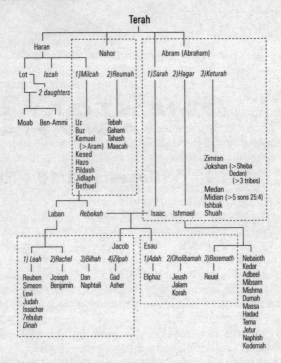

Different types of genealogy

In tribal societies, such as those in Genesis 5 and 11, genealogies that include only one name in each generation are called 'linear' genealogies, and usually serve the purpose of authenticating leadership. Those that include many people in each generation are called 'segmented' genealogies, and they serve several purposes:

▶ structuring society in terms of the functions that different families can perform;

▶ determining the rights of inheritance;

▶ providing guidelines for who can be married to whom.

The latter two reasons are crucial in Genesis, and we shall constantly be returning to them as we explore the stories of the patriarchs together.

Patriarchal marriages

It may be significant that in Terah's family tree there are exactly seventy males (or tribal groups) listed, forty-nine (7×7) of which are in Abram's branch of the family. What is more important is that the 'chosen' members of the family (Abram, Isaac, Jacob) marry *within* the family clan. This is called 'endogamous' marriage, and it usually occurs in tribal groups that wish to maintain their purity. The opposite (represented, for example, by Ishmael and Esau) is called 'exogamous' marriage, which normally occurs in tribes trying to build up alliances with other groups. When Abram moved to Canaan, there was a danger that Canaanite religious practices would engulf the family and drown out its knowledge of God. It was therefore important for God's chosen line to avoid marriage outside the clan (see, for example, Genesis 24:3–4).

We have to remember that this is for religious rather than racial reasons (compare 2 Corinthians 6:14). As it turned out, six of the future tribes have mothers who are not from Terah's clan: Bilhah and Zilpah are maidservants who become concubines of Jacob, and the mother of Ephraim and Manasseh is Asenath, the Egyptian wife of Joseph. Judah later marries a Canaanite (chapter 38), and the 'royal line' continues through his relationship with Tamar, his Canaanite daughter-in-law.

The latter example shows how complex relationships become in Genesis. Lot has a sexual relationship with his two daughters (19:30–38), Reuben with his father's concubine (35:22), Abraham marries a half-sister, and Jacob marries two sisters. The first two of these relationships were forbidden even in Genesis; the latter two are forbidden later (Leviticus 18:9, 18), but were acceptable during the patriarchal period.

The ages of the patriarchs

On pages 46–47 we discussed whether the ages recorded in chapters 5 and 11 were literal or symbolic. Although the ages in Genesis 12 – 50 are considerably smaller, they are still much larger than our normal experience, and the chronological information given makes a difference to the way we read the stories. It is easy from the text to construct a table giving the ages of the key characters at important points in the narrative; for reference, this is done on page 63. Ages given in the biblical text are in bold; the others can easily be calculated from these.

We see that generally the Genesis narrative is in chronological order, although the deaths of Abraham, Ishmael and Isaac are all recorded early in order to complete one section before a new story starts.

The ages given are important for appreciating the development of the plot. For example we need to know that Sarah is well past childbearing age in order to understand the magnitude of Abraham's faith; it is helpful to know that Rebekah is barren for twenty years before giving birth to Jacob and Esau; that Jacob is twenty years in Haran before being reconciled with his brother; and so on. Overall, the ages reached demonstrate God's protection of and blessing upon these patriarchal figures.

The figures also raise questions in our minds, however. It seems odd that Jacob fled from Esau at the age of seventy-seven, and that Laban, in chapter 29, is ninety-seven years older than in chapter 24. Likewise both Abimelech and Phicol must be about seventy years older in chapter 26:26 than in chapter 21:22–32. In addition, some of the figures do give the appearance of having a symbolic value. Most obviously:

▶ Abraham's life is dominated by multiples of 25: leaving Haran at 75, becoming the father of Isaac at 100, and dying at 175. (He is 150 when Shem dies at 600, 11:11.)

▶ Isaac becomes the father of Jacob and Esau at 60, and dies at 180 (3×60).

▶ Jacob marries Leah and Rachel, through whom will come the 12 tribes of Israel, when he is 84 (7×12), in the same year that Isaac is 144 (12×12).

▶ Joseph spends 17 years in Haran and Canaan with his father; later balanced by spending 17 years with him in Egypt.

► Jacob serves 7 years for Leah (who is fertile), and 7 for Rachel (who is barren); later there are 7 years of plenty and 7 of famine in Egypt.

ref:	Event	Abraham	Sarah	Ishmael	Isaac	Jacob Esau	Joseph
12:4	Abram leaves Haran	**75**	65				
16:3	Abram sleeps with Hagar	85	75				
16:16	the birth of Ishmael	**86**	76	0			
17:1	the promise of a son / circumcision	**99**	89	13			
17:17/21:5	the birth of Isaac	**100**	**90**	14	0		
23:1	the death of Sarah	137	**127**	51	37		
25:20	the marriage of Isaac	140		54	**40**		
25:26	the birth of Jacob and Esau	160		74	**60**	0	
25:7	the death of Abraham	**175**		89	75	15	
26:34	the marriage of Esau			114	100	**40**	
25:17	the death of Ishmael			**137**	123	63	
28:10	Jacob flees from Beersheba				137	77	
29:20	Jacob marries Rachel/Leah				144	84	
29:30/30:25	Jacob serves 7 more years, climaxing in the birth of Joseph				151	91	0
31:38	Jacob returns to Canaan				157	97	6
37:2	Joseph is sold into slavery				168	108	**17**
40; 41:1	the dream of the cupbearer and baker				179	119	28
35:28	the death of Isaac				**180**	120	29
41:46	Joseph enters Pharaoh's service					121	**30**
41:47	Seven years of abundance pass					120	37
45:6,11/47:9	Jacob enters Egypt after two years of famine					**130**	39
47:28	the death of Jacob					**147**	56
50:26	the death of Joseph						**110**

Other commentators have noticed that the ages of the patriarchs at their death form a mathematical sequence:

Abraham:	175 (7×5^2)
Isaac:	180 (5×6^2)
Jacob:	147 (3×7^2)
Joseph:	110 $(1 \times 5^2 + 6^2 + 7^2)$

This suggests that there may be more to these figures than immediately meets the eye. The figures are in the text, however, and in the absence of any alternative it is wisest to read the ages as given. In the commentary we have taken this approach.

The patriarchs and archaeology

There is no written record outside the Bible of the patriarchs. In the eyes of the ancient world they were, after all, just one family out of thousands of unimportant semi-nomadic wanderers, who by choice moved away from where civilization was flourishing.

It is reasonable, however, to place Abraham around the year 2,000 BC, within what is known as the Middle Bronze Age. The political alliances of Genesis 14 fit this period better than any other, and the various social customs that relate to the family (marriage within the family, the use of a slave-girl as a kind of surrogate mother, regulations regarding adoption and inheritance, burial rites, and so on) are compatible with what we know of that culture. This date also fits the internal chronology of the Bible, as the Israelites were slaves in Egypt around the middle of the second millennium BC.

Abraham

Abraham (whose name was originally Abram) is one of the key figures in the history of humanity. Both the Jews and the Arabs trace their ancestry back to him, and he is therefore revered in Judaism, Islam and Christianity. For Christians he is 'the father of all who believe but have not been circumcised' as well as 'the father of the circumcised' (Romans 4:11–12). We do not, however, have a 'biography' of Abraham. Other than the fact that he comes from 'Ur of the Chaldeans' (11:31) in southern Mesopotamia, and a few family details, we know nothing of his life up to the age of seventy-five, and little more than a dozen incidents subsequently.

Nevertheless these incidents build up into a well-rounded portrait. A morally strong man, with a concern for justice, he is prepared to live counter-culturally, setting his face against public opinion; but at times he can meekly give in to his wife. He is wealthy, with many flocks and herds, and an enormous household, but he chooses to live the life of a semi-nomad, based for years at a time in a particular area before moving on in response, for example, to political considerations or famine. He has the status and power of a local ruler, and when necessary can mount a lightning military attack, yet he always remains a resident alien in the land. He is usually courteous and dignified in his dealings with others, and intercedes with God on their behalf; but when he fears that they might harm him, he can also be deceptive and evasive. He makes major mistakes and sometimes acts without regard for the welfare of his family, but he is also capable of great repentance, seeking a new start in his relationship with God.

The thread that runs right through his life, though, is that Abraham is a man who, against all the odds, believes God. He comes from a polytheistic culture, and even his own father 'worshipped other gods' (Joshua 24:2); but somehow he hears the voice of the Lord commanding him to leave all of that behind and go to another country (12:1). He goes. His wife Sarah is barren and past the age for childbearing, but God has promised him a son and, in a stupendous act of faith, Abraham believes him (15:6). God's promise provides hope in the midst of a precarious existence, in which warfare, famine, infertility and personal failure all threaten to prevent the promise coming to fruition. When God later asks Abraham to give Isaac back, the old man is prepared to do so (chapter 22). These three acts of faith more than compensate for all his failures, and give him a place of honour in the 'roll-call' of faith in Hebrews (11:11–19), as well as being a model for Paul's understanding of what faith means (Romans 4).

Abraham's faith is in a God who acts in history, overturning the *status quo*, and subverting the normal order of things. When God decrees, the barren woman gives birth, the fertile plain becomes desolate, the firstborn son is displaced, and an Egyptian maidservant twice meets with him in the desert.

We cannot read the story of Abraham without our own faith being deeply challenged, but we also need to remember that Abraham's faith is the product of a lengthy walk with God. Although our own pilgrimage with God should also be characterized by a growing faith, this takes time, and we should not forget the many years in Abraham's life about which nothing is said, in which he is simply looking after his flocks and herds, caring for his family, and pondering God's words to him, allowing them to sink into his life, so that when the test of obedience comes, he is ready.

We should also remember that this is the story of Sarah, whose pilgrimage to faith is somehow more painful than that of her husband. She needs to work through a whole spectrum of negative emotions – frustration, resentment, jealousy and rage – in the context of a relationship in which she must wonder whether Abraham cares for her at all, putting her at risk and never telling her more than half the story. But the Lord's covenant is also with her, and she too is to be blessed and to be a blessing.

Structure

The stories we have about Abram/Abraham are arranged in a way that emphasizes the repetition of various themes (many of the stories reflect one another in various ways). The birth of Isaac, however, is a unique event, breaking into the latter part of the structure with nothing corresponding to it in the first half. Overall, the narrative pattern reflects Abraham's perspective, for until the birth of Isaac, the birth of Ishmael is *the* great turning point in Abraham's life, in which he truly believes that God's promises have been fulfilled.

A	The genealogy of Terah	11:26–32
B	The call of Abram; Abram's obedience	12:1–9
C	Abram puts Sarah in danger in Egypt	12:10–20
D	Lot moves to the plain of the Jordan	13
E	Abram rescues Lot	14
F	The covenant with Abram	15
G	The birth of Ishmael	16
F'	The sign of the covenant	17
E'	The angels rescue Lot	18 – 19:29
D'	Lot moves to the mountains	19:30–38
C'	Abraham puts Sarah in danger in Gerar	20
*	*the birth of Isaac*	21
B'	The testing of Abraham; Abraham's obedience	22:1–19
A'	The genealogy of Nahor	22:20–24

The remaining stories in the Abraham 'cycle' concern domestic matters: the death and burial of Sarah, the marriage of Isaac, the distribution of the inheritance among Abraham's sons and, finally, Abraham's death.

What did Abraham believe?

As a final caution, we need to guard against assuming that Abraham knew all that we know about the character of God. He had no Bible, and had only glimpses of what God had done in the past. He was a pioneer, paving the way for his descendants to have a greater knowledge of the one in whom he had put his faith. He explored different ways of expressing his faith: building altars, offering a tithe to Melchizedek (14:20), and planting a tree (21:33), as well as obeying the Lord in instituting the covenant of circumcision (chapter 17). If, at times, we feel that we can see things more clearly, we should never forget that we have had 4,000 more years of God's revelation – with the incarnation of God's Son equidistant between us. The faith Abraham had, given his background, was truly extraordinary, and as Christians we should not be ashamed to call him 'our father in the sight of God' (Romans 4:17).

Genesis 11:10 – 12:5

The heritage and call of a man of God

When God chooses a person to initiate a great work, he lays a firm foundation, giving that person an appropriate heritage, family situation and call.

This section introduces us to Abram, giving us important information about his family – the context within which God makes an astonishing promise to him.

From Shem to Abram (11:10–26)

This is a linear genealogy that branches out in the final generation. The line connecting Shem to Abram shows that Abram is, within God's purposes, the right man, with an appropriate heritage. But the mention of his brothers (verse 26) also indicates, as in 5:32, that the genealogy is about to branch out into a narrative. In this generation God is going to do something special!

The genealogical reports are shorter in form than those in chapter 5, indicating that the narrator sees them as being less important.

The family of Terah (11:27–30)

The relationships described in verses 27–29 can be seen more clearly in a diagram:

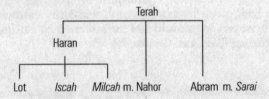

Notice that we are not told here that Sarai is a daughter of Terah, although in Genesis 20:12 Abraham says that she is his half-sister. What we are told is even more vital, as verse 30 moves us from genealogy to gynaecology: Sarai is barren. This simple statement casts its shadow over the next ten chapters, for if Sarai is barren, how can God fulfil his promises (12:2–3)?

From Ur to Canaan (11:31 – 12:5)

Ur, an ancient and prosperous city in the land of Sumer, was Abram's birthplace. It had considerable political importance, and at least 300,000 people lived there. The chief deity of the city was Nanna, the moon god, whom Terah's family would have worshipped (Joshua 24:2).

We do not know why Terah wants to go to Canaan (verse 31) unless Abram has already heard God's call (12:1), and Terah wishes to join him. However, when they reach Haran they stay there. This city – whose name is similar to that of Terah's dead firstborn son, although the Hebrew spelling differs slightly – also worshipped the moon god, and was an important trading centre. It must feel like a home from home, and Terah, at least, does not wish to go further.

Abram, honouring his family commitments, settles there until his father died (verse 32). But he never forgets his call, and at seventy-five, when the opportunity presents itself, he sets out with Lot and Sarai to venture beyond the borders of civilization (verses 4–5).

Abram also takes with him a word, a promise, a blessing from God with three components (verses 1–3). God will

▶ give them *a land* to dwell in

▶ give them *descendants*, and make their name 'great' (compare 11:4)

▶ *bless them*, and bless 'all peoples on earth' through them

These promises are not merely for Abram's benefit, but for the benefit of the whole human race; the rest of Genesis, and indeed the rest of the Bible, is an unpacking of these words.

Questions

1. In what situations might the command to 'honour your parents' (Exodus 20:12; compare 1 Timothy 5:4) be overtaken by 'kingdom' obligations (for example Luke 9:59–62)?
2. Churches sometimes measure commitment to God in terms of attendance at meetings, which makes those with demanding family or work obligations feel guilty. How can the church positively value and encourage such people?
3. Abram's family is more dysfunctional than we might imagine. In what ways does the church portray to society an unrealistic stereotype of the sorts of families that God blesses?

Rivalry and reconciliation between brothers

In the story of Cain and Abel (chapter 4), we saw that the Lord's approval of a younger son leads to conflict between brothers. This theme continues throughout the book. In each generation the Lord chooses to work through a younger son, for God – not human privilege, nor nature, nor human choice – is directing this story (compare 1 Corinthians 1:28). There is increasingly bitter conflict between brothers, however, as the firstborn is in some way deprived of the 'rights' normally expected within that culture. However, although the path to reconciliation is harder as the generations continue, in each generation the brothers *are* ultimately reconciled: Isaac and Ishmael (25:9), Jacob and Esau (chapter 33), and, most agonizingly of all, Joseph and his brothers (chapters 42 – 45). This pattern, obvious in the case of Isaac or Jacob, is also true in the less obvious cases of Shem and Abram.

In 11:10 Shem is 100 years old, two years after the flood. Noah is 500 when he first becomes a father (5:32); and 600 at the time of the flood (7:6). Ham is his youngest son (9:24). Thus Japheth is born first, when Noah is 500 (compare 10:21), Shem two years later, and finally Ham. (In 5:32 Shem is placed first simply because of his importance.)

Similarly with Abram. Abram leaves the city of Haran, aged 75 (12:4), after his father has died, aged 205 (11:32; compare Acts 7:4). Abram is therefore born when Terah is 130, sixty years after Terah first becomes a father at 70 (11:26). Presumably Haran is the oldest brother, as Nahor marries Haran's daughter (11:29), and Haran himself has died before they left Ur (11:28).

One implication of this is that Abram's nephew Lot, Haran's son, may be of a similar age to Abram himself. Abram can thus say to Lot, 'we are brothers' (13:8).

The dangers of being economical with the truth

It can often be tempting to hide or manipulate the truth by our own cleverness, but this usually leads to the problem getting even worse.

Abram has arrived in the land of Canaan. He travels through the land, but then faces his first major challenge: famine.

The tree and the altar (12:6–9)

Abram's first stop is 'the great tree' at Shechem, a town in central Palestine near Mount Gerizim. It is here, later in Israel's history, that Joshua renews the covenant (Joshua 24), and buries Joseph's bones (Joshua 24:32). Here also the kingdom splits into two under Rehoboam (1 Kings 12).

The great tree, significant in the Canaanite religion as a place where oracles are received, symbolizes the Canaanite possession of the land (verse 6). But Abram, in symbolic opposition to the tree, builds an altar (verse 7), for, in contrast, this is the land the Lord has promised to *his* descendants. Building an altar is the first stage of that possession.

Abram moves on, and builds another altar between Bethel and Ai (verse 8), before moving on again, symbolically possessing the land, and all the time heading towards the Negev desert in the south.

Too clever by half (12:10–16)

But Abram, the man of faith, quickly turns into Abram the man of fear. The cause is famine. When famine occurred in the area, as it frequently did, people would flock to Egypt, which had a more dependable harvest than elsewhere as its fields were irrigated by the Nile. On this occasion the famine is especially

71

severe (verse 10), and Abram joins the general drift towards Egypt, and out of the land.

It is hard to judge whether this shows a lack of faith (Abram does not seem to consult the Lord), or whether Abram is simply using his God-given wisdom to deal with a crisis. He clearly does sin, however, in trying to deceive and manipulate his hosts. Because of Sarai's beauty he is fearful for his life (verses 11–12), being unable to risk trusting the Egyptians to respect the marriage bond, or to trust God to keep his promises (12:1–3) – for they cannot come true if Abram is killed in Egypt! In his fear Abram pretends to be Sarai's brother, not her husband (verses 12–13), which is a half-truth (20:12), although completely misleading, and Sarai's barrenness, ironically, will make the lie more plausible. This will give Abram a position of power, as he can then negotiate a good bride price for his 'sister' (compare Laban in Genesis 24). Presumably he hopes to flee before any such negotiations go too far.

But Abram's cleverness rebounds on him: Pharaoh takes Sarai into his harem (verse 15) as his wife (verse 19). God's promise is now under serious threat, as Abram is out of Canaan, Sarai is in Pharaoh's harem, and Abram can hardly be a blessing to anyone. He is simply accumulating wealth (verse 16) and shame in equal measure.

We might, in passing, wonder whether Abram actually wants Sarai back. He shows little concern for her welfare, and as Sarai is a barren woman, whom he married before God called him, might he not be thinking that she is a hindrance to the fulfilment of God's purposes in his life? Is it not better for Pharaoh to have her, and for him to remarry? After all, the promises did not mention Sarai at all – and does not the wealth he is gaining indicate the Lord's blessing?

Leaving with his tail between his legs (12:17–20)

Whatever Abram is thinking, God's plans for the future certainly include Sarai – barrenness and all. And his plans for the present are to force Abram to drink the cup of humiliation, for 'the LORD disciplines those he loves' (Proverbs 3:12; Hebrews 12:6). When God calls us, he calls us as we are, and it may be that he will do his greatest work in those areas of our lives that we wish were different, or that we may even consider to be a hindrance in our service for him.

God finally breaks the deadlock by inflicting plagues on

Pharaoh (verse 17). It is not clear how Pharaoh links what is happening with Abram's deceit. Does he have a dream, or a prophecy? Does he sense Abram's embarrassment and put two and two together? Does Sarai confess? Perhaps it does not matter, or we would be told, but when he does make the connection, he angrily summons Abram and, instead of killing him (verse 12), simply gives him a verbal lashing and sends him packing (verses 18–19). Abram can say nothing in reply.

This humiliation must have lived long in Abram's memory, and his Egyptian possessions (13:2), gained under false pretences, must surely have pricked his conscience. Here was a man through whom God would bless all the peoples of the earth (12:3), who had failed abysmally at the first hurdle.

Abram's experience ironically foreshadows the later experience of Israel, who must have recounted the story to one another in Egypt with a sense of expectation – if God could bring Abram out, why not them? They have also gone into Egypt to escape famine (Genesis 46 – 47). Later they fear that their menfolk will be killed (Exodus 1:16), but eventually they escape with great wealth (Exodus 12:35), following a series of plagues (Exodus 7 – 11).

Returning to his roots (13:1–4)

In this situation Abram goes back, and then further back – through the Negev, 'from place to place until he came to Bethel … where he had first built an altar' (verse 3). Once more he calls on 'the name of the LORD' (verse 4). When we have failed we also ought to tread this route back to the 'Bethel' where we first met with God. Our footsteps, along with our voices, are praying, 'Lord, forgive; Lord, have mercy.'

Questions

1. How would you describe the difference between genuine wisdom and mere cleverness?
2. In what ways can your church 'build an altar to the Lord' to mark significant points in its spiritual pilgrimage?
3. In our own world what do you think constitutes a valid 'right' for a nation to possess a particular land?

Genesis 13:5–18

The hidden dangers of the easy option

Occasionally we are faced with decisions of such importance that they will influence the rest of our lives. In such moments it is often the more difficult option that proves to be best.

After the humiliation of the events in Egypt, Abram is given another chance to demonstrate his faith. The circumstance this time, however, is not famine but prosperity.

Abram's generosity (13:5–9)

We might imagine Abram with his wife, nephew and a few servants travelling the land as a small, vulnerable group. But in fact 'Abram plc' is a major organization with a large annual turnover, and employs hundreds of people; in 23:6 the Hittites describe him as 'a mighty prince' among them. Even allowing for oriental flattery, Abram is clearly a feared, or revered, figure. In 14:14 he sends out a military force of over three hundred trained men 'born in his household', so he must have been the head of a community of around a thousand people.

It is, then, all the more to his credit that he chooses to live the life of a semi-nomad rather than building a secure city, for he senses that such a life is more appropriate to his calling from God. The writer of the book of Hebrews tells us that 'he lived in tents ... For he was looking forward to the city with foundations, whose architect and builder is God' (11:9–10). He wants to be free to move, not just when his flocks demand it, but also when his walk with God, his spiritual pilgrimage, demands it.

By now Lot and Abram have both built up great wealth (verse 5). Not surprisingly, in a land of scarce resources, with each group needing access to pasture lands and water, quarrels break out between the herdsmen (verse 7). Inevitably, the groups have to separate before the situation becomes more serious (compare 36:7).

Abram has been wounded by his experience in Egypt, but his

humiliation has at least produced the fruit of humility. This time he is not going to use his human cleverness to obtain what God has promised him, nor to manipulate Lot in order to get the most favourable deal. Instead, in a dignified manner, he quietly lets Lot have first choice (verses 8–9).

Lot's choice (13:10–13)

The choice is simple: the Jordan valley, with its regular water supply and favourable climate, lies to the east (verse 10); the central highlands of Palestine, with their harsher climatic conditions, lie to the west.

Lot is not a wicked man. Indeed, 2 Peter 2:7–8 surprisingly describes him as 'that righteous man'. But he is weak and tends always to take the easier option. As he sees the Jordan valley his eyes conjure up comparisons with the Nile and the garden of Eden (verse 10). But he does not see that this garden also has its serpent, for the city of Sodom, with its reputation for wickedness, lies east (verse 13); and apart from the moral dangers, the valley is also a convenient route for an enemy army on the march. He does not know what the reader knows, that what looks 'good' and 'desirable' can lead to nakedness (compare 19:30–35), and death (3:6). Of course, he heads east (verse 11). But it will not be long before Lot wishes he were safely up in the highlands again.

God's promise (13:14–18)

Abram then receives, at last, a reaffirmation of God's promise to him (verses 14–17). He has been promised a land (12:1), but now his acceptance of the more difficult highland areas ironically works to his advantage. From the elevated position he can see further, and all the land he sees – north, south, east, west – God promises to give to his descendants (verse 15). Originally, these descendants were described simply as 'a great nation' (12:2); now they will be 'like the dust of the earth' (verse 16a). This image is then unfolded further (verse 16b), for, as we have already seen, dust can have negative connotations (compare 3:14, 19)! Abram is to walk through the land (verse 17), taking symbolic possession of it.

Finally, Abram moves once more, this time to Hebron, which will be his base for many years to come. He does not move south again until 20:1, just before the birth of Isaac.

Questions

1. Abram chose to 'live in tents'; in what ways might we symbolically demonstrate that our real home is not an earthly one?
2. Some churches seek to 'walk through' an area to claim it for Christ – is this a valid application of this story, or an abuse of the text? Why?
3. What promises that God makes in the Bible do you think are applicable to the worldwide church today, and what difference should this make to the way the church lives?

Genesis 14:1–24

Unexpected toughness

If we simply take the easy option, we may find ourselves in situations outside our control.

It is not long before the dangers of the Jordan plain become apparent, and Lot quickly finds himself in a situation beyond his control.

Lot ends up in trouble (14:1–12)

The fertile Jordan plain where Lot is living had attracted many other people as well: various small towns were scattered throughout the area. It was also a relatively easy region for armies to reach along the so-called 'King's Highway', which ran east of the Jordan Valley from Damascus down to the Gulf of Aqabah.

A number of years before, a certain Kedorlaomer, with his allies, came around the fertile crescent from Mesopotamia, and placed this region under his jurisdiction. After a dozen years of paying tribute, the local kings decide to rebel (verse 4), and when Kedorlaomer, together with his allies, come to take vengeance (verses 5–7), Lot is caught up in the ensuing battle. The local towns are defeated and plundered (verses 8–11); and

Lot, who has moved from pitching his tents '*near* Sodom' (13:12) to 'living *in* Sodom' (14:12), is taken into captivity and potential slavery (verse 12).

Abram to the rescue (14:13–16)

In a move that reveals a new side to his character, Abram leads a vigorous military attack on the departing forces. With an instinctive sense of battle strategy (was he a soldier as a young man in Ur?), he divides up his inferior force and attacked at night, a tactic later employed to equally good effect by Gideon with a similar-sized army (Judges 7:16–22). In addition, Abram calls on the help of his allies Aner, Eshcol and Mamre (verses 13, 24). The 'baggage train' is recovered and brought back, and Kedorlaomer and his allies flee back along the fertile crescent (verse 15). Abram has a genuine ongoing concern for Lot's welfare and, despite separating from him, never forgets him, and continues to pray for him (18:22–33; compare 1 Samuel 12:23).

Dividing up the spoils (14:17–24)

On his return from battle Abram meets the king of Sodom (verses 17, 21–24) and, more importantly, the king of Salem (verses 18–20). We can learn something from each of these encounters.

Abram deals with the king of Sodom in a cursory way. He first ignores him in order to meet Melchizedek, and then dismisses the king's suggestion (that Abram should keep the booty) with an oath. All he claims are his travelling expenses and the share that belongs to his allies (verse 24). He does not want the king to boast that he has 'made Abram rich' (verse 23). The Egyptian experience is surely still at the back of his mind, as Pharaoh can indeed have made that claim (12:16). Abram, though, has learned from that experience, and his refusal now to gain any wealth from the king of Sodom is perhaps something of an atonement for his earlier sin.

His encounter with Melchizedek, the king of Salem (presumably Jerusalem) is far more significant and mysterious. Clearly here we have a deeply spiritual man from outside the covenant community. He knows God, although only as the Creator, and as 'God Most High' (verse 19). What takes place indicates that he is in some way Abram's superior: this 'priest of God Most High' (verse 18) gives bread and wine to Abram, with his blessing (verses 19–20), and in return Abram gives him 'a tenth of everything' (verse 20).

Questions

1. If you were to pray for the well-being of those with whom you disagree, who might you be praying for?
2. In the light of Abram's example, what circumstances are there in which your church would refuse to accept grants or other donations towards, for example, a building fund?
3. How might we assess whether someone who is not a part of the Christian church nevertheless has a real, although limited, knowledge of God – and may even, in some ways, be spiritually superior to us?

Melchizedek

This tantalizing story is the only mention of Melchizedek in Genesis. Later, after David captures Jerusalem, the title Melchizedek held seems to be applied to him (Psalm 110:4), but of greater significance is the connection made in the New Testament between Melchizedek and 'David's son', Jesus.

Thus the writer of Hebrews (quoting Psalm 110:4) describes Jesus as 'a high priest ... in the order of Melchizedek' (Hebrews 6:20). To connect Melchizedek with Christ (Hebrews 7:2–3) the author plays on the meaning of Melchizedek's name and title, and on the fact that we are not given his genealogy. He then uses the fact that Abram offered tithes to Melchizedek to symbolize the superiority of Jesus' priesthood over that of Levi, Abram's great-grandson (Hebrews 7:4–10), and ultimately the superiority of the covenant Jesus established over that established with Moses (Hebrews 8).

As a second point of contact we might also wonder whether Jesus has this story in mind when he gives 'bread and wine' to his disciples, Abram's descendants (Mark 14:22–23). The Gospels, however, never make this connection and therefore we can but speculate.

We are called to live by faith in God, but God in his graciousness often gives us visual aids and experiences that reinforce his promises to us.

 Abram has begun to live a 'life of faith' in Canaan, allowing Lot the best of the land (chapter 13) and refusing the economic benefits of an alliance with the king of Sodom (14:22–24). But the original promise (12:2–3) still seems far from being fulfilled – and Abram is not getting any younger.

God's presence (15:1)

As so often in Scripture, when God speaks, his first words are words of reassurance: 'Do not be afraid … I am your shield' (verse 1). Abram may have good reason to be afraid on a human level: having refused the reward offered by the king of Sodom (14:22–24) he might now be regarded as an enemy. The Lord, however, in this vision at night, promises Abram his own presence, as both protection and reward (verse 1).

Not a servant, but a son (15:2–6)

But Abram has the courage not to be content with what, in certain situations, might appear to be a platitude. Real faith always speaks its mind to God, who delights in such a robust challenge. 'How long, O LORD, must I call for help, but you do not listen?' cries Habakkuk (Habakkuk 1:2). 'O LORD, you deceived me, and I was deceived' says Jeremiah (Jeremiah 20:7). Job speaks words about God that frighten the more fragile faith of his friends, but it is Job who speaks 'what is right' (Job 42:8).

In response to God's words, Abram cries out, 'what can you give me since I remain childless …?' (verse 2). After a pause, when no reply comes, he says again, 'You have given me no

79

children; so a servant ... will be my heir' (verse 3). Eliezer is a responsible, trusted servant, who (presumably) is the one later commissioned to find a wife for Isaac in Genesis 24, but he is still a servant, not a son.

If we never complain, how can God console us? And Abram is consoled, as the promise is clarified: No, Abram, not a servant, but a son. And not just a son, but ... look at the stars, Abram – 'So shall your offspring be' (verse 5). God's purposes for us are always much bigger than we can imagine (compare Ephesians 3:20–21)!

And, wonder of wonders, Abram believes him (verse 6). Something mysterious happens within Abram that day that brings his relationship with God on to a new footing; one of friendship. This is a verse Paul can't get out of his mind when he struggles to describe what happens when a person becomes a Christian (Romans 4:3, 22). We must also put our faith in the promise of God, which finds its meaning and fulfilment in Christ, who was also 'not a servant, but a son' (paraphrasing Hebrews 3:5–6). We too, in our turn, become sons and not servants, 'heirs of God and co-heirs with Christ' (Romans 8:17).

The promise of the land (15:7–21)

The Lord now brings up the topic of the land (verse 7), and once again Abram desires reassurance (verse 8). There then follows what looks like a bizarre ritual: Abram cuts a young cow, a goat and a ram in two, and places the halves opposite each other, together with a bird on either side. Not surprisingly, as the day continues, birds of prey try to attack and have to be driven off.

This, however, will all have made sense to Abram. It was typical of a ritual in his day that bound two nations together in a covenant relationship. Leaders of the two states would walk between the pieces, binding themselves with an oath that if they broke the agreement they were willing for their country to become like the carcasses they had walked between. (For another example of this, see Jeremiah 34:18–20.) It is typical of God that he speaks in a culturally relevant way, in, as it were, Abram's 'mother tongue'.

As the sun sets, a blanket of darkness falls upon Abram, and he hears that the promise about the land is one he will not live to see; it is for the future: 400 years (verse 13), or four long generations (verse 16), will first pass.

And then in the darkness he sees fire and smoke, symbols of

the presence of God (compare Exodus 13:21; 19:18), or perhaps symbols of God and Abram, moving between the carcasses. God himself, in the most solemn way possible, covenants with Abram that the land, although now occupied by ten tribes (verses 19–20), will be a gift from him to Abram's descendants.

Questions

1. What situations are there in your life in which you need to hear God's reassuring words 'Do not be afraid'?
2. When you pray with other Christians, how can you make sure that there is the psychological space for people to challenge God, as well as to praise him?
3. What would you say to someone who argued that modern-day Israel had the right to hold all the land – as far as the Euphrates – which was promised to Abram?

Genesis 16:1–16
God's promise is fulfilled – or is it?

If God has promised us something, and an opportunity develops that enables us to speed up the fulfilment of that promise, should we take it or not?

Abram's relationship with God seems to be going well. He has believed God's promise that he will have a son, but he has now been in Canaan ten years. Is it not time to do something more proactive that will enable the promise to be fulfilled? Sarai certainly thinks so!

Hagar, the surrogate mother (16:1–6)

If a woman could not have a child, and did not want her husband to take a second, younger, wife, it was quite normal to give her slave-girl to her husband, and any child born would be

counted as her own. This enabled the family name to be continued and the inheritance to be dealt with smoothly.

We must also remember that God had never specified who
the *mother* of Abram's son was going to be. There have been no
promises from God for Sarai, only the dead weight of barrenness and the realization that childbirth is now too late. Sarai
imagines that God has no place for her in his plans, and chooses
what seems the only option left:. she gives 'her maidservant' to
her husband (verse 2). Note that neither Sarai nor Abram use
Hagar's name, for in their eyes she is simply a means to an end,
and not a person in her own right. But if God has no purpose for
Sarai's life, why did he rescue her from Egypt (12:17)?

Abram agrees to Sarai's request, and sleeps with Hagar (verse
4), who becomes pregnant. The problem with playing God is
that we can't see the knock-on effects of our actions. Soon the
dominoes start falling … Hagar sees Sarai through new eyes,
and begins to despise her. Sarai blames Abram, who washes his
hands of the whole business (verses 5–6a). And then in a small-
scale reversal of the exodus story, Sarai ill-treats the Egyptian
Hagar (verse 6b; the same word is used in Exodus 1:11–12), who
then flees (as do the Israelites in Exodus 14:5) as far as Shur
(verse 7; compare Exodus 15:22). Sarai's smooth plan of verse 2
has suddenly become completely derailed. And this family,
whose calling is to bring blessing to the earth, has succeeded
only in becoming a community of oppression.

Meeting the angel of the Lord (16:7–14)

Hagar (no doubt one of the slave-girls acquired from Pharaoh in
12:16) decides to return to Egypt. But at one of the springs in the
Negev she hears her *name*, and then two questions: Where have
you come from? Where are you going? These are two of the
simplest, but also most profound, questions we can ask, and we
can answer them at many different levels. If God were to speak
our name, and ask those two questions, what would we say?
Hagar sensibly tells the truth about where she has come from;
but it is the angel who answers the second for her, with a hard
command: Go back, submit (verse 9).

Perhaps the angel sees the fear on her face, for, after a pause,
he gives her a promise as well. Like the promises to Abram, it
begins with the big picture: 'you will have many descendants'.
But it quickly narrows down to the one child she is carrying:
'You shall name him Ishmael' (verse 11). The child will not have

an easy life (verse 12), but Hagar now has the strength to go and do what God requires, for she has met with God, and knows that he is watching over her (verse 13).

Abram the proud father (16:15–16)

Abram does not come out of this story with a lot of credit, having acted rather feebly so far, but at least he believes Hagar's story. After the birth, it is thus Abram who names the child (verse 15), indicating his willingness to take on the responsibilities of fatherhood. At the age of eighty-six, he holds a newborn son in his arms! The circumstances may not have been ideal, but at least, and at last, he has a son, and he can hardly get over it. How he is going to love this son! Surely God has fulfilled his promise!

But what of Sarai? The child, after all her plans, is Hagar's, and not hers. And it is Hagar, her Egyptian slave-girl, who has received a promise and has seen the Lord. Abram and Hagar have each had an experience of God denied to Sarai. Yes, there is a baby crying in the tent at night, but for Sarai there is no comfort in this – only bitterness. Finally, we might wonder whether Hagar ever told Abram that the angel had mentioned that Ishmael would have 'brothers' (verse 12).

Questions

1. Ask each person in the group to answer, for themselves, the two questions Hagar faced: 'Where have you come from?'; 'Where are you going?'
2. How can your church best support those of its members who have to live for years, and perhaps decades, with unfulfilled desires and unanswered prayers?
3. How should Christians respond to the ethical dilemmas involved in surrogate motherhood?

Genesis 17:1–27

Cut off – or be cut off

It is good to have symbols that remind us of our relationship with God, but we must never forget God's desire for an inward transformation.

Years go by, and, as Abram watches Ishmael grow, he becomes more and more convinced that this is, indeed, the promised son. Until one day, a year short of his hundredth birthday, he once more meets with God.

Reaffirming the promises (17:1–8)

It is thirteen years since Abram has heard God's voice. Now God confirms what he said previously. Notice again the various elements of the blessing:

▶ *An ongoing relationship with God.* God again confirms that he will keep his side of the covenant (verses 2, 7), and will be not just the God of Abram, but also of his descendants (verses 7, 8).

▶ *Land.* Again, Abram is assured that the land of Canaan will come into the possession of his descendants (verse 8).

▶ *Descendants.* This is reinforced again and again: God will increase his numbers (verse 2), Abram will be the father of many nations (verses 4, 5, 6) and will be very fruitful (verse 6), with 'generations' of descendants to follow (verses 7–8).

As a sign of these promises, Abram's name is to be changed from Abram ('exalted father') to Abraham ('father of many'). No doubt this will cause his neighbours some merriment, but, as so often, a change of name indicates what a person is to become, not necessarily what they are. It takes Peter a long time to become a 'rock' (Matthew 16:18)!

The sign of the covenant (17:9–14)

As the covenant with Noah (9:8–11) was followed by 'the sign of the covenant' (9:12–17), so too the covenant with Abraham (15; 17:1–8) is followed by the giving of a sign. God has confirmed that he will keep the covenant, and in response he expects his people to keep their side. Ultimately he wants an inward transformation: 'Be holy because I, the LORD your God, am holy', he later tells the Israelites (Leviticus 19:1). For now, however, he tells Abram the requirement is simply an external, symbolic one: they are to circumcise all the males in the community. If they are not 'cut off' in the flesh, they will be 'cut off' from the people (verse 14). The symbol seems to imply that as a community they are 'separated' for God's purposes. It may also denote that to be truly God's people, the patriarchal domination of the community needs to be 'cut off' – it is a result of the fall (3:16), not a mandate from God. Either way, it will be a permanent reminder for them of their covenant obligations.

Circumcision was practised by other ancient peoples (see Jeremiah 9:25–26), but Israel seems to be unique in circumcising babies. In most cultures it was an adolescent rite of passage into manhood. The circumcision of children, however, demonstrates God's graciousness to the people: they are born into a covenant relationship with him, rather than having to 'earn' their place.

The bombshell (17:15–22)

God now makes a third speech to Abraham. His wife's name is to be changed to Sarah, and she is to bear a son, her own son, who will be called Isaac. And as Abraham is to be the 'father of many nations' (verses 4, 5), so, too, Sarah will be the 'mother of nations', and kings will be among her descendants (verse 16; compare verse 6). God's covenant will be with Sarah as well as with Abraham. He has never forgotten Sarah, but he waits silently until the right moment. In times when you feel rejected by God, when everyone else is having spiritual experiences that you seem to be missing out on, remember Sarah. The time may come when God does something in your life that puts others to shame, when 'the stone the builders rejected', once more 'becomes the capstone' (Psalm 118:22). But God may first test your patience beyond its breaking point.

For many years now Abraham has perhaps assumed that Sarah has no part in the promise, that she is simply baggage to be carried over from his past life, before his call, rather than the means of fulfilling God's promise in the future. But if God's words are true, then Abraham has been wrong all along: wrong in his attitude towards Sarah, wrong in his actions with Hagar, and wrong in his assessment of Ishmael, his firstborn. Thus Abraham doesn't really want God's promise to be true, but wonders if it might be, and so he laughs, neither with joy nor with unbelief (although these may coexist; see Luke 24:41), but at the incongruity of it all. Doesn't God know how old they are (verse 17)? Surely Ishmael is adequate?

But God insists that his promise will not be fulfilled in a second-best way. The mother, as well as the father, will be his choice, not theirs. There will indeed be a blessing for Ishmael (verse 20), for throughout Genesis God blesses the 'unchosen' line. The Cains, Ishmaels and Esaus of this world do still live under God's 'creation blessing' (compare verse 20 with 1:28); they have human success and political independence, but the covenant is another matter. That is a matter of God's choice, and it is Isaac, Sarah's son, with whom the covenant will be established (verse 21).

Abraham's immediate obedience (17:23–27)

'On that very day' (verse 23) Abraham obeys God's command – obedience is always all the better for being an immediate response. Every male in the household is circumcised, from the ninety-nine year old Abraham to the thirteen-year-old Ishmael to all the servants.

Questions

1. What should our response be when God is silent and appears to be putting us to one side?
2. How can we prevent Christian symbols (such as baptism and communion) from degenerating into mere ritual?
3. The Christian church has often adopted pagan customs and given them a 'Christian' content (for example Christmas). What do you think are the opportunities and dangers in this process?

How long is an everlasting covenant?

Several times God states that his covenant is an 'everlasting' one (verses 7, 8, 13, 19). How we understand this word is important for our attitude, for example, to modern Israel. Does she still have the theological right to 'the whole land of Canaan' on the basis of verse 8?

The Hebrew word translated 'everlasting' is *olam*. This refers to 'distant ages' either in the past (for example Deuteronomy 32:7; Proverbs 22:28) or, more frequently, in the future. However, it does *not* contain the idea of 'endlessness', despite the NIV translation. Jeremiah, in talking about this covenant, can argue that God would one day make 'a new covenant with the house of Israel' (Jeremiah 31:31); and the writer of Hebrews, in commenting on Jeremiah, notes that this implies that the old covenant is obsolete and will 'soon disappear' (Hebrews 8:13).

The same word is used to describe the rite of circumcision (verse 13). In the early church many Jewish Christians thought that Gentile converts ought to be circumcised (Acts 15:1, 5). The (Jewish) church leaders and theologians, however, argued against this (see Paul's arguments, for example, in Romans 2:25–29; 4:9–12; Galatians 5:2–6), for the *olam* covenant of circumcision, which had lasted 2,000 years, had come to the end of its term of office.

Thus the covenant itself, and the sign of the covenant, find their 'end' and are transformed in Christ. There seems good reason to assume that the same applies to the promise of the land (verse 8). This promise has been transformed for God's people into the gift of the Spirit, the 'land' in which they must now walk (Romans 8:4 RSV) and whose fruits they must bear (Galatians 5:22–23). It is true that in terms of natural justice and human rights the nation of Israel has a right to its own land, but this should not be backed up by appealing to Genesis 17; and justice equally demands that the rights of others should not be trampled upon when searching for a solution to the problems of that region.

Genesis 18:1–33

An unexpected after-dinner speech

God's people are called to be models of hospitality, of faith and of intercession.

Once more the Lord appears to Abraham. Three men arrive, and Abraham offers them lunch.

Abraham the model host (18:1–8)

Abraham has been living 'near the great trees of Mamre' since he and Lot separated, probably over twenty years previously (13:18). As would be his normal custom, he is sitting at his tent's entrance during the hottest part of the day, but when he sees three strangers, he immediately offers them hospitality (verses 3–5).

Hospitality is crucial in a country where the offer of shade, water and food might, for some travellers, make the difference between life and death. Even in less extreme circumstances, a meal together established a relationship, and relationships were at the heart of Near Eastern culture. (Notice how often Jesus builds relationships with people by having meals with them.) Abraham would have seen it as a privilege to offer this service, and in a flurry of activity hurries to organize a meal for them (verses 6–7), which he serves himself (verse 8).

Sarah is let in on the secret (18:9–15)

Visitors are always welcome sources of news in a nomadic or semi-nomadic culture. But rather unexpectedly this visitor asks a question about the whereabouts of Sarah, using her recently changed name (verse 9). Assured that Sarah is within hearing distance, the visitor repeats the promise made earlier to Abraham, that within a year Sarah will bear a son (verse 10; compare 17:16–21). Abraham realizes that these are no ordinary visitors, but the Lord himself with two accompanying angels are his guests (compare Luke 24:30–31; Hebrews 13:2).

The conversation is intended to get a response from Sarah, for she is nervously hiding, much as Eve earlier hid among the trees (3:8). When she hears the promise of a child, perhaps for the first time (we do not know whether Abraham ever told her what the Lord had told him in 17:16), she also laughs at the incongruity of the thought (verse 12). The Lord repeats Sarah's inward thoughts to Abraham (verse 13; tactfully leaving out the comment about Abraham's age, verse 12), and again confirms the promise (verse 14). He also challenges Sarah's laughter, and finally provokes her into a defensive response (verse 15). But she is lying, and this too is challenged, for she must not deny her laughter of incredulity if it is to be transformed into the laughter of joy (21:6). The Lord never rebukes honesty – it gives him space to work.

Abraham the model intercessor (18:16–33)

If the meal continued, no doubt the atmosphere was somewhat strained. However, at last the guests get up to leave, and Abraham, ever the courteous host, shows them on their way (verse 16).

The Lord then explains to Abraham the secondary purpose of his visit: to 'test' Sodom and Gomorrah. How will they respond when two strangers visit their town? As 'the Judge of all the earth' (verse 25) it is right not just to act fairly, but to be seen to be doing so. Before this, there is a monologue that indicates the Lord's growing friendship with Abraham. Abraham will become a key figure in the Lord's plans for humanity (verse 18), even though for the first time it is hinted that those plans are partly conditional upon Abraham guiding his family in the right direction (verse 19; compare 26:5), and therefore he is to be allowed 'inside information' as to what some of those plans are (verse 17; compare Amos 3:7).

The Lord then waits (verse 22, NIV footnote) in order to see whether Abraham shares his own concern for justice (verse 21). One is 'the Judge of all the earth' (verse 25), the other, 'dust and ashes' (verse 27). But their concern for justice binds them together and, much as Amos later prays for mercy upon a people doomed to destruction until it is clear that his praying should stop (Amos 7:1–9; compare verse 8), so too Abraham prays for Sodom. The 'hidden agenda' of his prayer, though, is Lot, perhaps the one 'righteous' man in the city.

But Abraham begins by trying to establish a basic principle:

will the Lord 'kill the righteous with the wicked' (verse 25)? Supposing there are fifty righteous? Note that the Lord never directly answers the first question – there have been many times in the history of the world when, indeed, the righteous have been killed with the wicked; and once when the most righteous one of all was killed, and 'assigned a grave with the wicked' (Isaiah 53:9). But for fifty? No, the Lord will not destroy Sodom for the sake of fifty.

What about forty-five? Forty? Thirty? Twenty? Ten? No, 'For the sake of ten, I will not destroy it' (verse 32).

Abraham dares not go lower, and leaving he returns home (verse 33), no doubt heavy in heart, to await further news.

Questions

1. Why are we often reluctant to be hospitable to strangers, and how can we encourage one another to overcome these barriers?
2. What lessons about intercession can your church learn from Abraham's example?
3. In many disasters the 'righteous' *are* killed with the 'wicked'. How would you defend the statement that 'the Judge of all the earth' is doing right?

Genesis 19:1–29

Flee for your life!

God's judgment hovers over those who abuse others, and half-heartedness in fleeing from it may not be enough.

In Genesis 6 – 8, God destroys a whole population, due to their endemic evil, while rescuing one righteous family. The same pattern is repeated on a smaller scale here.

The threat of Sodom (19:1–11)

In verses 1–2 there is a deliberate parallel with the beginning of chapter 18. As Abraham is sitting at the entrance to his tent, so Lot is 'sitting in the gateway of the city' (verse 1). Lot, like Abraham, goes to meet the strangers, and offers them hospitality. Lot is not a wicked man, but is 'righteous' and 'tormented ... by the lawless deeds' he sees and hears (2 Peter 2:7). In this chapter he is even prepared to be counter-cultural enough (in the eyes of his neighbours) to protect visitors to the town, and it may have been his normal custom to watch out for such people.

Lot never has the moral authority of an Abraham, however, and the angels at first refuse his invitation. After eventually accepting, and eating a simple, hasty meal (verse 3) – in contrast to Abraham's lavish feast (18:6–8) – Lot's worst fears are realized: the house is besieged by a violent crowd wanting to gang-rape the guests (verses 4–5). Any form of sexual abuse, forced intimacy, or unilateral imposition of your will upon another, is an evil and is worship of the false gods of lust and power. (Compare how delicately the Lord treated Sarah in the previous chapter.)

Lot tries to rebuke and appease the crowd by desperately offering them his daughters (verses 6–8), perhaps to shock them into their senses, but they simply taunt and threaten him. His words carry no authority, and Lot himself needs to be rescued – by his visitors, who shut the door on the chaos outside (verse 10; compare 7:16). The angels then physically blind those who are already blind at the deepest level of their being.

We may think that such sins could never happen among God's people, but Judges 19 shows that they can, and did. These stories are written, not for us to self-righteously judge Sodom, but to guard against becoming like Sodom ourselves.

Flee! (19:12–22)

It is never clear who was crying out to the Lord against the inhabitants of Sodom (verse 13; compare 18:21). It may have been people who had been victims of the evil prevalent within the city, or it may even have been the land itself. In Genesis 4:10 the same verbal root is used to describe Abel's blood crying out to the Lord from the ground. Even when there are no witnesses, there is a protest from within the fabric of creation, an outcry in the ears of God, against evil.

Lot's weakness is again demonstrated. His sons-in-law think

he is joking (verse 14). He needs to be manhandled to safety by his visitors (verses 16–17), and tries to avoid having to run too far (verses 18–20). The angels allow him this request also (verses 21–22).

Sodom goes up in smoke (19:23–29)

When the Lord brings judgment, he usually uses the tool that comes most readily to hand, rather than relying totally on 'supernatural' means. In the case of Sodom and Gomorrah, which we know were in an area of bitumen, or 'tar pits' (14:10), within the system of the Rift Valley that extends down into East Africa, 'burning sulphur' was the appropriate instrument of divine anger. It may have been that the Lord caused noxious gases released in an earthquake to ignite, but we will probably never know. Whatever happened destroyed both the cities and the vegetation, which is ironically what had attracted Lot to the area in the first place (13:10). This demonstration of divine judg ment functioned as a warning for Israel (Deuteronomy 29:23) and for Jesus' own generation (Matthew 10:15), and should function likewise for us today (Jude 1:7).

'Remember Lot's wife!' the Lord commands his disciples (Luke 17:32). Most of us remember her (if at all) for turning into a 'pillar of salt' (verse 26), but of course Jesus' focus is on the first part of the verse (verse 26a). Lot's wife is an example of someone who, with the path leading towards safety in front of her, looks back, showing that her heart, after all, is still in Sodom. After escaping from Egypt, the Israelites too are condemned for hankering after what they have fled from (Numbers 11:4–6), and as Christians we are constantly exhorted to look forwards rather than backwards (for example Philippians 3:13–14).

The narrator beautifully takes us away from the close-up shot of Lot's wife to the panoramic view that Abraham has the next morning, but all Abraham now sees (in contrast to 13:10 and 18:16) is dense smoke rising from the ground. This is an image that haunts the poetic imagination: Tolkien uses it to describe the land of Mordor in *The Lord of the Rings*, and John uses it as a picture of 'the second death' in Revelation (14:10–11).

Abraham's prayer for Lot is, after all, answered – God indeed 'remembered Abraham' (verse 29), much as he earlier 'remembered Noah' (8:1). The city has not been saved – there were not ten righteous people within it (18:32) – but Lot has been rescued, yet again, this time by angels rather than by his uncle (compare chapter 14). Unlike Rahab (Joshua 6:25), who will later be rescued from another city destined for destruction, Lot is unable to bring out his whole household, but at least he has been rescued, albeit 'only as one escaping through the flames' (1 Corinthians 3:15), together with his daughters. But will anyone be able to rescue Lot from the emotional collapse that follows?

Questions

1. 'Looking back' may be either a positive or a negative reaction. How would you distinguish between the two?
2. In what ways can we watch that great sins do not erupt within the heart of our own church community?
3. What criteria might we use to assess whether a disaster has any element of God's judgment within it?

Genesis 19:30–38
Spiralling out of control

A righteous but weak man who refuses to take his family responsibilities seriously may easily spiral downhill into a degrading moral collapse.

 This section tells us of the ancestry of the Moabites and Ammonites, two people groups who lived east of the Jordan River and who were frequent enemies of Israel in later years. But it is also the final, sad story of a potentially righteous man who has unwisely allowed himself to drift further and further away from his godly heritage and calling. As you read, listen again for echoes from the story of Noah (9:18–23).

The daughters' plan (19:30–32)

In many ancient societies (as in many modern societies) women had limited rights of appeal. A woman's responsibility was to obey her father until she married, and subsequently to obey her husband. It was the father's responsibility to ensure that a daughter found an appropriate husband so that the family 'line' would be continued.

After the destruction of his adopted home town, the death of his daughters' fiancés, and the death of his own wife, Lot collapses inwardly. He can no longer bear to live in the small town of Zoar, and instead retreats with his daughters to a cave in the mountains. Perhaps today we would describe him as suffering from post-traumatic stress disorder, or diagnose the guilt people feel when they alone have survived a major disaster. But nevertheless, he is surely still responsible for his actions. Lot's responsibility is now to find other husbands for his daughters, but all he wishes to do is to flee from the memories of Sodom, from Zoar, and from any further responsibilities in life.

The daughters therefore are the ones who must act to continue the family line, fulfilling the creation mandate of 1:28 and 9:1. The way they do this is shocking, but how else can their voice be heard? We should not judge them, for we have never been in their situation. We would do better to learn to give the oppressed a voice, and to 'Speak up for those who cannot speak for themselves' (Proverbs 31:8), than to sit in judgment on these unnamed daughters, or on those who feel compelled to act like them.

Again, there is a sense that Lot receives poetic justice, for he had offered his daughters to the brutal men of Sodom (verse 8); and now he is taken advantage of by those same daughters. Given Lot's own refusal to accept responsibility, he can hardly complain.

The plan is successfully carried out (19:33–38)

On two successive nights the plan is carried out, and each of the daughters becomes pregnant. Their family line *is* thus continued, but whether for good or for ill, only the unfolding story will reveal.

Questions

1. In what situations might an 'unethical' action be acceptable in the pursuit of a higher purpose?
2. Do you think your church would judge the sin of Lot or the sin of his daughters more severely? Explain your reasons.
3. How do you think women should act in societies where, in the eyes of the law, they are oppressed, exploited and silenced?

Can anything good come out of Moab?

There is no sin so dark that God cannot bring some good out of it – however many generations that may take. If you read the book of Ruth, you discover the close links between this story and that in Genesis 38 of Judah sleeping with his daughter-in-law Tamar.

In all three of these stories people who have been bereaved of both spouse and sons (or sons-in-law) face the responsibility of providing for the future of their daughters (or daughters-in-law). Lot and Judah both ignore their responsibility, and in these cases the women have to resort to devising strategies for sleeping with their father (or father-in-law), without his knowledge, in order to gain some semblance of justice. Naomi, in contrast, does her best to find husbands for both Orpah and Ruth.

As we read Ruth, it is important to remember that (1) Ruth is a Moabitess, descended from the union of Lot with his older daughter, and (2) Boaz, Ruth's potential husband, is descended from the union of Judah with his daughter-in-law Tamar (Ruth 4:18–22). Thus in Ruth 3 there is a re-enactment of the situation facing the characters in Genesis. Ruth meets a slightly inebriated Boaz alone in the middle of the night, and we wonder to ourselves whether either is going to follow the example of their ancestor (or ancestress) and seduce the other. Or will they refuse the easy option and act as people who have committed themselves and their future to God?

The choice they make is recorded in Ruth 3 – 4. They do not need to be bound by the examples of their ancestors, for a relationship with God can break the power of sin, even of sins deeply rooted within a family tradition. Being born into a dysfunctional family may leave a person bruised, as many of us may have experienced, but it need not leave us bound, inevitably repeating the past. And God can use the bruises to help us touch the lives of others with similar hurts.

Ruth and Boaz receive God's blessing in their lives as a result of their obedience. Israel too receives blessing, as Ruth and Boaz's great-grandson is King David. Amazingly, the blessing extends even to us, as each of these characters also features in the genealogy of Jesus (Matthew 1:5). Can anything good come out of Moab? Within the grace of God – yes!

Genesis 20:1–18

Fear and failure

Even the greatest of God's servants can, under pressure, repeat the same mistake more than once.

Faith and fear alternate in Abraham's life (compare Elijah in 1 Kings 18 – 19). After his original act of faith in moving to Canaan (12:5), he fears for his life in Egypt (12:10–13). Now, after his prophetic intercession for Sodom (18:16–32), he again faces a pagan king.

Moving home (20:1–2)

Abraham has lived near Hebron for about twenty-five years, almost all the time that he has been in Canaan. After the devastation of Sodom and Gomorrah it is time to move on. The fertility of the land may have been affected by the devastation, or perhaps the ruined cities are too sombre a reminder to have constantly on the horizon. For a while Abraham adopts a semi-nomadic lifestyle in and around the Negev desert, which brings him into the territory around Gerar, a town in the west of the Negev. There seems little real direction in his movement, as if he has somehow lost his way, and perhaps his vision. The destruction of Sodom seems to haunt him; and when he stays in Gerar, he again meekly says that Sarah is his sister, a relationship Sarah confirms (verse 5). Once again she is taken into the harem of a pagan king (verse 2). On this occasion no mention is made of her beauty (12:11, 14), which has presumably faded with the stresses of the previous quarter-century. The taking of Sarah, this time, is purely a political move, establishing a potential alliance between two powerful figures.

It should not be forgotten how awkward a moment this is in the story. Sarah has been promised a son 'within a year' (17:21; 18:14), and this son is not yet born. We cannot help asking whether she is pregnant yet. If she is in Abimelech's harem, will there be future question marks over the paternity of the child? But enough time goes by for it to become apparent that none of the females in Abimelech's household is falling pregnant (verse 18).

God's warning to Abimelech (20:3–7)

Abimelech is the innocent party in this deception, and God's speech to him (verse 3) sounds, to our ears, rather harsh. However, the speech sets the agenda for the conversation, rather than being the final word – it invites a response. Abimelech protests his innocence (verses 4–5), paralleling Abraham's own appeal to God not to destroy the righteous (18:23). God acknowledges Abimelech's innocence, confirming for us in passing that Abimelech is *not* the father of any future child of Sarah's (verse 6). God's original statement is now modified: now that Abimelech knows the truth of the situation, punishment will only fall upon him if he fails to return Sarah to Abraham (verse 7).

God's judgments *are* modified according to the knowledge of those upon whom they fall. All mitigating circumstances will be taken into account, including those we ourselves are unaware of. Nevertheless, we each have a core of responsibility before God for our actions; and warnings of judgment should not be lightly put to one side. They are intended to provoke a response of repentance.

Abraham's explanation and intercession (20:8–18)

In Egypt Abraham was scolded like a schoolboy and dismissed (12:18–20), but on this occasion, he and Abimelech are of a similar status, and Abimelech demands an explanation (verses 9–10). But Abraham's excuses are all so feeble that we have to wonder what he thinks he is doing. He is afraid (verse 11); but he could call out 318 'trained men' to rescue Lot (14:14), defeating 4 kings in the process! If it comes to a fight, he must at least be the equal of Abimelech. But does he *really* believe that his life is in such serious danger from someone desiring his ninety-year old wife that it is better simply to *give* her away, just before she is due to conceive a child to fulfil God's promises? This is so ridiculous that one wonders whether this is a final attempt by Abraham actually to *prevent* the promise coming true, so that Ishmael will remain as his heir (17:18).

Abraham also argues that his statement was half true (verse 12) – but half-truths frequently repeated (verse 13) might be more dangerous to our spiritual health than the occasional downright lie!

Abraham expects to find godlessness in Gerar, but in fact his own lack of spirituality is shown up by Abimelech. The king and his officials fear God and act with nobility in giving gifts to Abraham – whom Abimilech refers to, in an extremely barbed way, as Sarah's 'brother' – and in allowing him to remain where he chooses (verses 14–16; compare 13:9), presumably now with the status of a 'resident alien' (compare 23:4).

Despite his failure, Abraham is still a prophet (verse 7; compare Romans 11:29), and when he prays, God heals Abimelech (verse 17), so that his household can again have children. Abraham may have considered this somewhat ironic given the many decades Sarai has been barren; but this, too, is about to change.

Questions

1. What half-truths are we in danger of telling to ourselves or to others?
2. What needy situations are there in your local neighbourhood about which your church might develop a prophetic ministry of intercession?
3. How can Christian leaders guard against developing the perception that others are somehow less godly than they actually are?

Genesis 21:1–34

Naming the future

As we learn to see things as God sees them, we can name them in a way that reminds us of his faithfulness in the past and his promises for the future.

Abraham accepts Abimelech's offer of land (20:15; 21:23), remaining there 'a long time' (21:34). During this time Abraham both gains, and loses, a son.

At last: Unto us a son is born (21:1–7)

The time of waiting is over: God does as he has promised (verse 1; compare 17:16) – at the very time he has promised (verse 2; compare 17:21; 18:14) – and a child is born to Sarah. Much later, of course, the pattern is repeated: God again does what he promised (Acts 13:23), at the right time (Galatians 4:4), and another child is miraculously born.

Abraham names his child Isaac (verse 3; compare 17:19) and circumcises him on the eighth day (verse 4; compare 17:12). The birth of 'Isaac' (the Hebrew means 'he laughs') transforms Sarah's laughter from the laughter of uncertain incredulity, in which she sees her body as being 'worn out' (18:12), to a contagious, public act of astonishment that she can again 'nurse children' (21:6–7; compare Psalm 126:1–3).

Another son is sent away (21:8–21)

As so often, the positive is followed by the negative. Sarah's faith is still fragile: she can laugh with Isaac (verse 6), but can't cope with Ishmael laughing at him (verse 9). And she fears that Ishmael may share the inheritance (verse 10). Despite his misgivings, with God's confirmation that this is the lesser of two evils (verses 11–13), Abraham agrees to send his son away and to trust that God will care for him. The emotions Abraham goes through are no doubt a dress rehearsal for the greater sacrifice

99

God will ask him to make when Isaac is a little older (22:2).

From Hagar's point of view it is better to be sent away legitimately with provisions and with her son, than to flee while pregnant (16:6). Nevertheless Hagar and Ishmael quickly discover the harsh reality of life in the desert when they run out of water, and prepare to die (verses 15–16). In a strange way Hagar earlier foreshadowed Israel's exodus; now she foreshadows their exile. (In Paul's theology, she represents Israel itself: Galatians 4:24–25.) She weeps in a strange land, with no direction home, but once more the Lord meets with her, providing the water she needs (compare Isaiah 43:19–21), and giving her hope for her future: her son's tears have been heard (verse 17), and he will be the founder of a great nation (verse 18).

Hagar, in her own way, is a hero of faith. She accepts the need for suffering, first in returning to Sarah (16:9) and then in leaving (verse 14), so that the covenant promise is transmitted smoothly to another generation – but not to her son, begotten through the schemings of two other human beings, and now rejected by them. As a single parent she brings the child up in a grim environment (verse 20), even taking on the father's role in finding a wife for the lad (verse 21). And God, as he has promised, watches over the boy (verse 20). Once again, God's graciousness extends to those who are not the 'chosen people', and especially to those who are humanly vulnerable. He is concerned for their life and future, hearing their cry, giving them his blessing and dwelling with them. He opens their eyes to the resources they have, and gives them the space to develop skills for survival. Of all people, God's people ought to be the ones who demonstrate a similar care for the whole of humanity.

The elder of Abraham's two sons faces death in a desert, only to be reprieved by an angel calling from heaven at the last moment (verse 17). We ought not to be surprised, in the next chapter, when Abraham's younger son encounters a similar threat.

A treaty and a tree (21:22–34)

Abraham is living in the territory governed by Abimelech, and as usual in desert areas there are disputes over water rights (verses 25, 30). Abimelech and Abraham both wish to maintain peaceful relations, and the two men therefore make a treaty (verses 27, 31), which provides a framework within which the water disputes can be sorted out peacefully (compare Hebrews

12:14). And it must encourage Abraham that Abimelech recognizes that God is with him (verse 22), despite his earlier mistake, and that he is beginning to be a blessing to others (compare 12:3).

As a reminder of the treaty, the place is named 'Beersheba' (verse 31). This becomes an important location in the northern Negev, marking the southernmost limit of agriculture in Palestine. As a reminder that God has given him this place, with the blessing of the local ruler, Abraham plants a tree (verse 33; compare Psalm 1:3), for he now has roots in the land himself; his son has been born there, and he has the rights to a well.

Questions

1. In verse 10 Sarah calls Hagar 'that slave woman'. What names, nicknames or derogatory terms do we use to reinforce our prejudices about others, and what alternatives might we use to give us a truer picture?
2. What occasions in the life of your church community could be celebrated by 'planting a tree' as a reminder of God's goodness to you?
3. God is gracious towards all who are vulnerable, whether they are his people or not. What vulnerable groups might you seek to help as a witness to this aspect of God's character?

Genesis 22:1–19

The greatest test

Do we love God more than anything or anyone else?

God tests the faithfulness of his servants at the beginning and at the end of their lives. At the beginning he asks, 'Are you willing to walk in my ways?' and at the end, 'Are you willing to give everything back? Do you love *me* more than the things I have given you?'

Daniel defies a royal command both as a teenager (Daniel 1:8) and in his eighties (Daniel 6). Jesus' greatest temptations are at the beginning (Mark 1:12–13) and end (Mark 14:32–42) of his ministry. When first called, Abraham 'obeyed and went, even though he did not know where he was going' (Hebrews 11:8). And now God asks him to go on another journey, and to give up his son, his only son, whom he loves: Isaac (verse 2).

The preparation (22:1–8)

Jehoshaphat and Isaiah both describe Abraham as 'God's friend' (2 Chronicles 20:7; Isaiah 41:8). But what sort of a God asks his 'friend' (or anyone!) to sacrifice a child? Of course, Abraham would not have had the same cultural revulsion to the idea of human sacrifice as we do today; it was common in many ancient societies. But we know that child sacrifice is abhorrent to God's very nature. Why then does he ask Abraham to sacrifice Isaac?

One answer might be that God always meets people where they are. He therefore works *within* Abraham's cultural framework in order to bring to the surface the depths of Abraham's faith. Wisely, unlike 21:11, the narrator does not try to describe Abraham's feelings. He simply describes his obedience – the quiet preparation for the burnt offering and the 45-mile journey to Mount Moriah (verses 3–4) that would take three days. He also hints at Abraham's faith, however. Abraham tells the waiting servants, '*we* will come back to you' (verse 5); for 'Abraham reasoned that God could raise the dead ...' (Hebrews 11:19). He then gives the wood to Isaac, and carries the more dangerous objects himself (verse 6). As we see father and son walking together up the mountain, each burdened in his own way, we catch just a fragment of their conversation (verses 7–8), and in his reply, Abraham speaks more truly than he knows.

The answer to our original question 'What sort of a God would ask his friend to sacrifice a son?' is this: only a God who is prepared to sacrifice *his* own son, whom *he* loves. God himself provides the lamb (verse 8; compare John 1:29). And it is only natural that words from this passage are echoed by 'the voice from heaven' when Jesus is baptized (see Mark 1:11). As God, a father himself, would go through the agony of sacrificing his own son, so Abraham, God's friend, is given the chance to share God's agony of heart. Paul prays for the privilege of 'sharing in his sufferings, becoming like him in his death' (Philippians 3:10). Is this is a prayer we would want to repeat?

The substitute (22:9–19)

Abraham builds an altar (verse 9). Previous altars (12:7, 8; 13:18) have symbolized God's promise for the future, as Abram walked through the land; this one indicates Abraham's willingness to relinquish any personal control over that future.

Isaac, able to carry the wood up the mountainside (verse 6), must be at least a young teenager. No doubt he could easily escape and flee from his elderly father, but he deliberately chooses not to, consenting to what will happen by silently allowing himself to be bound (verse 9; compare Isaiah 53:7). And, as so often in this story, we again hear the distant echo of a much greater Son, also choosing to carry the wood and refusing to escape his Father's will. In that later story, as in the story of Jephthah's daughter (Judges 11:34–40), there is no last-minute reprieve, and the angels do not intervene (compare Matthew 26:53). In our story, though, as with Ishmael (21:17), the angelic voice comes in time (verses 11–12); and a ram is provided instead (verse 13).

Abraham names the mountain 'The Lord Will Provide' (verse 14); later, it significantly becomes the site of Solomon's temple (2 Chronicles 3:1). Abraham then hears a more passionate confirmation of the blessing, perhaps because he has now demonstrated his worthiness for it (verses 15–18), for although some of God's promises may be unconditional, he still desires his people to act in a way worthy of them. Finally Abraham returns to the servants (verse 19), before going back home. We might well wonder what he tells Sarah.

Questions

1. Think about those whom you love. How would you feel if the Lord wanted you to let go of them, for example, into full-time Christian work overseas?
2. How do the characteristics of Abraham, God's friend, compare with the image of a 'successful Christian' presented in your church, or in the Christian media?
3. Abraham's willingness to sacrifice his son brought blessing to 'all nations on earth' (verse 18). In what ways have you been blessed through the sufferings of Christians elsewhere in the world?

Genesis 22:20 – 23:20

Domestic duties

Spirituality can be demonstrated just as much in day-to-day family affairs as in moments of supreme sacrifice.

We can't always live on the spiritual heights. After Abraham's commitment to God has been dramatically demonstrated, he goes home; and the only stories left to be told are domestic ones. He receives news of his  brother's family; Sarah dies, and he needs to buy a burial ground (chapter 23); he needs to find a wife for his son (chapter 24); and after his remarriage he sorts out the inheritance (chapter 25). But these stories are not an anticlimax, for by these actions Abraham is laying the foundations for God to work in future generations as well as in his own life.

The sons of Nahor (22:20–24)

This small genealogy separates the two most emotionally draining events in Abraham's life: the near-sacrifice of his son and the death of his wife. However, it also gives us glimpses of the future. Nahor married within the family (11:29) and had been blessed by God; will God not bless Abraham's descendants if they do the same? Rebekah, who will later be Isaac's wife, is mentioned here for the first time (verse 23). If God can give twelve sons to Abraham's brother (eight by a wife and four by a concubine), will he do any less for Abraham's grandson (Genesis 29 – 30)?

The death of Sarah (23:1–2)

Again, decades go by, during which we are told of no further experiences of God. At some stage Abraham moves from Beersheba back to Hebron, where he had lived for many of his early years in Canaan (13:18). Sarah dies here (verses 1–2), and Abraham mourns the loss of his lifetime companion.

The cave of Machpelah (23:3–20)

Abraham, a lifelong pilgrim, has never held the title deeds of any land. After being in Canaan for over sixty years, he still describes himself as 'an alien and a stranger' (verse 4). Now that Sarah's pilgrimage has come to an end, however, Abraham desires to purchase a plot of land as a permanent resting place for her, and as a further act of faith that God will give the whole land to his and her descendants. He therefore approaches the Hittites (compare 15:20) with this request.

The whole debate is conducted in public in a typically courteous oriental fashion, with a good deal of flattery, where what is implied is frequently more (or less) than what is stated. Abraham wants to buy land, with little concern for the price; he might have haggled with the Lord over Sodom (18:22–33), but it is beneath his dignity to haggle with Ephron over the price of a burial plot for his wife. The Hittites, for their part, are happy to *give* him land – which will put Abraham under a certain obligation to them – but less happy to *sell*, which will change the legal status of Abraham from a 'resident alien' to a legal landowner.

In the first exchange (verses 3–6) Abraham makes his request; the Hittites respond by offering to give him the best of their tombs, which, although sounding generous, is not what Abraham desires. In the second exchange (verses 7–11) he builds on what the Hittites have conceded, and requests a particular cave from Ephron. Abraham's concern, though, is still to *buy* the cave, but in return Ephron offers to *give* it to him, together with the field as well. Presumably the unrequested field is thrown in either to increase Abraham's indebtedness to the Hittites, if they do give it to him, or to increase the price if it comes to a sale, although Abraham must sense that it is apt for Sarah to lie among living trees (verse 17) as well as in a barren cave. Again, though, what sounds like 'a bargain' is not necessarily the best long-term option.

Finally, Abraham forces Ephron to name a price (verses 12–16). Ephron asks for 400 shekels – and it is either a very high price, or a very large field – with a shrug that suggests it is almost beneath his dignity to haggle over a price. In comparison, Jeremiah pays only 17 shekels for a field (Jeremiah 32:9); and David only 50 for a threshing floor and some oxen (2 Samuel 24:24). Ephron may deliberately be putting Abraham into a no-win situation: either Abraham pays a highly inflated price, or loses dignity by negotiating a lower one. In the same dignified way that Abraham refused to accept a gift from the king of Sodom (14:22–24), he simply accepts the price named – possibly embarrassing Ephron in the process. He publicly weighs out the 400 shekels of silver, and gains legal possession of the land (verses 17–18).

The whole land of Canaan has been promised to Abraham by God (13:14–17), but at the end of his life he owns only this field, and the rights to a well (21:30). Similarly, he is promised many descendants, but at the end of his life he has only one son in the chosen line. Nevertheless it is a beginning, and to those like Abraham who have faith, great things happen from small beginnings. But the greater the faith the greater the timescale over which God may choose to work.

Questions

1. Our materialistic society constantly tempts us with 'bargain' offers, which are usually in the seller's interests rather than ours. How can we learn from Abraham to maintain our dignity in such matters?
2. How can your church give people the space to mourn and weep in times of bereavement?
3. What foundations should we be laying for God to work in future generations of the worldwide church?

Genesis 24:1–67

The next link in the chain

There is always a balance between praying for the Lord's overruling, and using our own common sense, when seeking guidance.

Isaac, in his late thirties (25:20), is unmarried. He is still attached to his mother and is deeply affected by her death (24:67b). Abraham feels that this is a good time for his son to marry.

Commissioning the servant (24:1–9)

For Abraham, Isaac's marriage has more than usual significance. Of course, like any father, he wants his son to settle down, but in this case God's promise of descendants depends on Isaac's marriage, as it is with Isaac that the covenant has been established (17:19, 21). Isaac's wife has to be a very special person, as her descendants will be God's chosen family. Thus Abraham does not want Isaac to marry a Canaanite girl (verse 3) who would be worshipping her own gods. This is not prejudice, but simple wisdom (compare 2 Corinthians 6:14–16).

Abraham knows that his brother Nahor has a granddaughter, Rebekah (22:23), but there are no doubt other suitable women within the family. He therefore commissions his chief servant (presumably Eliezer, mentioned in 15:2) to find a wife for Isaac (verse 2). The seriousness of this mission is shown by the need for a solemn vow (verses 2, 9). To allay the servant's anxiety (verse 5), he gives him instructions on what to do – and what not to do – if the mission fails (verse 8).

The meeting at the well (24:10–27)

Guidance is never easy, especially in a matter as important as marriage. The servant, rather sensibly, does three things. He prays (verse 12), he goes at the right time to where the local girls congregate (verse 11), and he thinks through what sort of a woman will make a good wife for Isaac. She must be a hard worker, gracious towards strangers, hospitable, able to take the initiative, and good with camels (verse 14)!

Rebekah enters the scene … and the narrator tells us she is a member of Abraham's wider family (verse 15), and is a virgin (verse 16). The girl is also very beautiful (verse 16), a bonus the servant has not asked for, but which might have tempted him to go to her first with his request (verse 17)! She gives him a drink, and everything seems to be falling into place; but despite the promising beginning, the servant is wise enough not to jump to conclusions – it can still all go wrong. He watches her closely (verse 21) as she waters the ten camels (compare verse 10) – no mean feat, for a thirsty camel after a long desert journey can drink up to 25 gallons! He then asks about her family (verse 23) and requests hospitality. Finally, on receiving the reply he has been waiting for (verses 24–25) – she is, in fact, descended from *both* of Abraham's brothers – he worships the Lord (verses 26–27).

Telling the story to Laban (24:28–51)

In an eastern culture, the family's approval was needed before a marriage could take place. Laban, the brother, is immediately attracted by the man's obvious wealth (verse 30), and Laban plays the leading role within the family (compare verses 50, 53, 55).

The servant is offered hospitality and food, but first recounts the reason for his visit. His speech (verses 34–49) more or less follows the earlier account (verses 3–27), but, no doubt quick at observing the family's priorities, he emphasizes Abraham's wealth (verse 35), all of which Isaac will inherit (verse 36), and also the element of divine providence in the event, which leaves Laban and Bethuel with little choice but to accept the offer (verses 50–51).

Rebekah accepts the proposal (24:52–67)

The servant stays the night (verse 54), but then wants to move on. The two members of the family who have received 'costly gifts' from him (verse 53) want him to stay longer (verse 55), perhaps in the hope of getting more or perhaps to give them time to say goodbye properly. In the end Rebekah decides the issue, and with her consent and their blessing they leave immediately (verses 58–61). The blessing (verse 60) echoes the blessing on Abraham in 22:17, reinforcing our sense that she is the correct bride, one who, like Abraham himself, is willing to leave her family and travel to a distant country.

Isaac marries Rebekah, and loves her (verse 67), taking her 'into the tent of his mother Sarah' and being 'comforted after his mother's death' (verse 67). And we might wonder, as we leave them together: does Isaac really love Rebekah for who she is? Or does she merely fill a hole in his life? Is this truly a relationship that will flourish, or will it eventually die?

Questions

1. What practical advice and help can your church give to those who are struggling with their singleness?
2. Given the high rate of divorce in Western society, what can the church do to demonstrate the seriousness of a marriage commitment?
3. What can we learn (both positively and negatively) from cultures in which parents take greater responsibility for arranging the marriages for their children?

3

THE STORY OF JACOB

Genesis 25 – 36

Stop and look

The second half of the book of Genesis is dominated by the figure of Jacob. Chapter 25 recounts his birth, and chapter 50 his burial. The later chapters (37 – 50) focus on Joseph, and it is helpful to deal with them separately; but while Joseph is in Egypt we should never forget that Jacob is still alive and mourning for his favourite son back in Canaan. But the real formation of Jacob's character occurs in the events recorded in chapters 25 – 35.

We meet Jacob as he is being born, already clutching the heel of his brother (25:26)! Clearly the Lord will have a hard task to shape this man into one of his servants. Yet in these stories the Lord takes a step backwards, and although he promises Jacob protection, Jacob has to learn his lessons the hard way. When Abraham meets the Lord it is midday, and they have lunch together; when Jacob finally meets the Lord it is midnight, and they wrestle with one another until the dawn.

Jacob is a character people can relate to easily. He has obvious sins that need to be dealt with, and there are clues to help us interpret his inner life. When he is angry, or in love, or favouring one person rather than another, the whole world knows about it.

Jacob is gradually transformed during the course of the narrative. Not, perhaps, as much as we would like – he never quite gets rid of his favouritism, which causes so much damage to his family – but the wisdom and dignity of his last years in Egypt are far removed from the passionate battle of wits with Esau and then with Laban. Although much of his suffering is self-inflicted, caused by his ambition and favouritism, at least he allows it to mould him. Ultimately, however, he is changed by seeing God 'face to face' (32:30) and by wrestling with him in the darkness. He walks away from that encounter with a limp, but also with a sense that something deep inside has changed. The rumour of God has become a reality for him at the core of his life, and this is perhaps why we turn back to this story: we too, at a certain level, desire to grasp hold of God and not to let him go until he has blessed us, even if we are wounded in the process. We, too, would like to be Jacob.

Structure

The narrator has arranged the stories about Jacob around the framework of his journey to Haran and back. At the central point lies the birth of Jacob's sons, because, although the wrestling match with God is the climax of Jacob's personal spiritual journey, in terms of the ongoing fulfilment of God's promises the most significant act is the birth of the heads of Israel's twelve tribes. This begins the population explosion that transforms God's chosen line into his chosen people, and begins to make sense of his promise that Abraham will become 'a great nation' (12:2).

A	The birth of Jacob and Esau	25:19–26
B	Jacob gains the birthright	25:27–34
C	Isaac and Abimelech, a local ruler	26
D	Jacob's deception and flight	27 – 28:9
E	Meeting God at Bethel	28:10–22
F	Arriving in Haran	29:1–14a
G	Jacob's wives	29:14b–30
H	Jacob's children	29:31 – 30:24
G'	Jacob's prosperity	30:25–43
F'	Leaving Haran	31
E'	Meeting God at Peniel	32
D'	Jacob's return to Canaan	33
C'	Jacob and Shechem, a local ruler	34
B'	Jacob gains God's blessing	35:1–15
A'	The deaths of Rachel and Isaac	35:16–29

Notice how Jacob's encounters with God at Bethel and Peniel neatly balance one another (E/E'); and how both Jacob and his father have significant dealings with local rulers (C/C'), although with Isaac this leads to a peace treaty, and with Jacob it leads to a massacre. Finally, the section ends, not with the death of Jacob (for his life will continue through most of the Joseph narratives) but with the deaths of his wife and father. Isaac's death has been brought forward in the narrative as a neat way of concluding this section; it does not occur chronologically until after Joseph is in prison in Egypt.

Genesis 25:1–34

Brothers!

The end of a life provides the opportunity for a reconciliation, but there will always be another generation to sow more seeds of conflict.

This section completes the cycle of stories about Abraham and begins a new cycle whose focus is Jacob. Abraham's death brings Isaac and Ishmael closer together, but the theme of 'rivalry between brothers' is about to step up a gear: Rebekah's twins begin their jostling early, while still in the womb (verse 22).

The final days of Abraham (25:1–11)

Abraham has done all he can to ensure that God's chosen line will continue. His son's wife is barren, but it is now Isaac who must learn to pray, and to develop his own faith (verse 21). As if the burden of his life has been lifted, rather unexpectedly Abraham remarries, and has another six sons (verse 1). Abraham's last act is to distribute his wealth, and he leaves everything to Isaac (verse 5). In compensation, gifts are given to the other sons (verse 6), reflecting, perhaps, the gifts God himself gives to the various 'unchosen' lines throughout Genesis.

After living a hundred years in Canaan (verse 7; compare 12:4), Abraham dies. He is reunited with Sarah in the cave of Machpelah and his sons join together to bury him (verse 9).

The sons of Ishmael (25:12–18)

The genealogy of the unchosen line – that of Ishmael – is summarized before the narrator focuses our attention on the chosen line. In addition, if God can fulfil the minor prophecies with regard to Ishmael (16:11–12; 17:20), how much more will he fulfil his purposes for the chosen family? Note the pattern that repeats itself: Abraham's brother has twelve sons (22:20–24), but Abraham's wife is barren; Isaac's brother also has twelve sons, and Isaac's wife is also barren (verse 21).

Unidentical twins (25:19–26)

Isaac's prayer for his barren wife, and the answer, are placed side by side in verse 21; but twenty years go by before the prayer is answered (compare verses 20, 26). The wait is shorter than Sarah's, but for a childless couple it is long and painful enough, in the light of her family's blessing (24:60).

Rebekah discovers that she has twins (verse 22); and in the message she receives from God, she learns that each will become a nation, but 'the older will serve the younger' (verse 23). Once again, the same themes emerge; God's choice of the younger son is a counter-cultural one, but to what extent should the younger son take steps to ensure the fulfilment of the promise? And how will the older son react?

Even the birth foreshadows aspects of their future. Esau, the firstborn, is hairy and will grow up, like Nimrod (10:9), to be a hunter (verse 27); Jacob, the younger twin, is grasping Esau's heel (verse 26), symbolizing his determination to grasp what Esau has – the rights and the blessing given to the firstborn.

Jacob wins the first round (25:27–34)

Despite his miraculous birth, the glimpses we have of Isaac always suggest a rather immature figure; perhaps as the only child of rich, elderly parents he never had the conflicts needed to grow into maturity. Everything was handed to him on a plate. He did not need to work through a potentially difficult relationship with an older brother, for Ishmael was sent away (21:14); and he did not even woo his own wife – she simply appeared over the horizon on a camel (24:63)! Now, as an old man, he is preoccupied with food, especially Esau's cooking (verse 28). Perhaps while eating he can ignore the fact that his family is terribly divided: his twin sons despise each other (verse 27), and the parents favour different sons (verse 28).

Jacob, by nature, is a calculating opportunist; and although it may have been prophesied that he will have the upper hand, he sees nothing wrong in ensuring that the prophecy will come true! His brother comes in, desperate for food. 'Let me gulp down some of this red, red stuff ... ' would be a more accurate translation of verse 30. Whether Esau is simply famished, or (as some have suggested) suffering from hypoglycaemia (low blood sugar), is irrelevant to Jacob, who sees his chance. He easily manipulates his twin into giving him the birthright (verse 33); and then waits for the opportunity to manipulate his father into ratifying the agreement with his blessing (chapter 27).

Thus, whereas Jacob tries to grasp what the Lord has promised to give him, Esau despises what he has already received – but neither model is an edifying one!

Questions

1. What do people mean when they warn about the danger of 'losing our birthright' as Christians, and how can we guard against this?
2. It is right that church leaders will have closer relationships with some than with others, but how can they guard against a destructive 'favouritism'?
3. Abraham, a 'father of many nations' (17:5), is a revered figure in Judaism, Islam and Christianity. What do you think he would say in response to both the strife and the attempts at dialogue between the various branches of his offspring?

Genesis 26:1–33

In his father's footsteps

When we model ourselves on another person, we need to ensure that we make their faith our own, and that we do not repeat their mistakes.

The stories about Isaac in this chapter closely, and significantly, parallel stories about his father Abraham:

event	Abraham	Isaac
receiving a promise from God	12:1–3	26:3–5
obeying instructions about where to stay	12:4–9	26:2–3a,6
famine	12:10a	26:1
pretending that his wife is a sister	12:10b–20	26:7–11
gaining great wealth	13:1–4	26:12–15
giving way in a dispute over land	13:5–13	26:16–22
receiving confirmation of the promise	13:14–17	26:23–24
building an altar	13:18	26:25
making a treaty with Abimelech	21:22–34	26:26–31

As we go through them, it may be helpful to 'compare and contrast' the way that Abraham and Isaac dealt with the similar situations they faced.

Gerar revisited (26:1–11)

Isaac was the only patriarch who lived his entire life within the promised land. Whereas his father refused him permission to move north (24:6, 8), the Lord now refuses him permission to move beyond the southern border (verse 2). Isaac does, however, travel to the southernmost border to avoid the famine (verse 1), territory controlled by Abimelech. The treaty between Abraham and Abimelech (21:22–31) may have encouraged Isaac to hope to find hospitality there.

At this stage the Lord reiterates to him the promises made earlier to Abraham: blessing, land and descendants (verses 3–5). It is important for Isaac to develop his own relationship with the Lord; as so often in godly families, it is easy for children to grow up with an adopted, second-hand version of their parents' faith. Despite this reassurance from the Lord, however, Isaac's fear gets the better of him, and the father's half-truth (20:12) becomes the son's lie (verse 7). By now Abimelech is weary of strangers claiming to be accompanied by 'sisters', and there is no attempt to bring Rebekah into the royal harem, despite her beauty (verse 7). The king no doubt keeps a close eye on them, presumably giving them land near his own palace. When the truth is revealed (verse 8) the king again summons the offender (although with more resignation and less passion than earlier;

compare 20:8–10), and asks for an explanation. After the by-now-standard reply, he, rather than Isaac, acts to preserve the integrity of Isaac's household (verse 11).

The search for a space (26:12–33)

Isaac seems less affected by his failure than his father ever was, and perhaps this is what makes him a lesser figure. He simply gets on with life again and, astonishingly, the Lord blesses him with wealth (verse 13), thus demonstrating that he can indeed look after Isaac in the promised land, despite the famine. This provokes the jealousy of the locals (verse 14), forcing Isaac to move back to an area his father had cultivated (verses 16–18). Isaac then needs a new water supply, but the first two wells he digs provoke quarrels, and so he leaves them – whether due to timidity, embarrassment that he had prospered more than his hosts, or faith that the Lord will provide, is unclear. On the third occasion he is left in peace and settles down (verses 19–22).

Like his father he now receives a confirmation of the promise and builds an altar (verses 23–25). Abimelech acknowledges that Isaac has been blessed by God (compare 21:22), proposes a treaty, and leaves in peace (verses 26–31). The blessing is further demonstrated by the discovery of another water supply (verses 32–33).

Is Isaac truly a good model for us? His whole life has been lived as a pale reflection of his father. He has been blessed by God, true, and perhaps he is content with that – but he doesn't really know God. When we next meet him, almost half a century later, he is simply a sad, blind, old man about to be duped by his youngest son.

Questions

1. Who are our role models, and how can we avoid repeating their mistakes?
2. How can your church move on from simply being content with God's blessing?
3. In what ways can God's blessings on a society hinder that society from turning towards him?

Genesis 26:34 – 28:9

Blindness, deceit, agony, flight

Sometimes God's plans come to fruition in the midst of a context in which everyone is working simply in their own interests.

In chapter 25 Jacob gained the birthright from his brother Esau. Unless this was ratified by their father Isaac when he gave his farewell blessing to his sons, however, it would not be worth a great deal; and Isaac is planning to give the blessing to Esau.

The wives (26:34–35; 28:6–9)

The story significantly begins and ends with the wives of Esau. In 26:34–35 Esau marries two Hittite women, and we immediately sense that he will not be the one to continue the chosen line. Earlier he valued his need for food above his birthright (25:32); now he marries outside the family clan, despite the examples of his father and grandfather. Esau is a loner, acting in his own self-interest rather than in the interests of his family, and he has no insight into what God requires. In marrying two women, his actions parallel those of Lamech (4:19); and in planning to murder his brother, he parallels the character of Cain (4:8). At the end of the story he tries to make amends by marrying a woman from the family, but chooses the daughter of Ishmael (28:9), himself an 'unchosen' older brother who had also forfeited the firstborn rights to a younger brother. Esau has found his niche – but within the darker, shadow side of this complex family.

Biblical characters are rarely straightforward. Jacob is a scheming, deceitful trickster, but for all his faults, there is something about him that God can mould. In contrast, however much we may sympathize with Esau's momentary anguish (for example 27:34), we know that he can never be a patriarch. Esau hunts animals (25:27), looks like one (25:25), and eats like one (25:30), whereas Jacob dreams of angels (28:12). And that makes all the difference.

The plan (27:1–17)

Isaac is physically blind (verse 1); but he is also blind to what God is doing. He ought to be more open to going against tradition and giving the blessing to the younger twin (25:23), for he was a younger son himself. Esau, though, has been his favourite for too long, and so Isaac, like his hunter-son, acts ignorantly, and in his own self-interest. In exchange for a meal he decides to give his death-bed blessing to Esau (verses 1–4) – a case, perhaps, of like son, like father.

In 25:28 we saw that Isaac and Rebekah each preferred a different son. This had now escalated into a major rift between them. In this chapter, until verse 46, Isaac and Rebekah never speak to one another. Indeed, Rebekah, on the basis of the oracle she received (25:23) – which is also in line with her own pref-erence – acts in a way that thwarts both the plan of her husband (verse 4) and then the plan of her eldest son (verse 41) in order to serve the interests of Jacob.

Jacob is reluctant to go along with her scheming, although only because he fears getting caught (verses 11–12). His mother, though, reassures him and prepares the food (verse 14), disguis-ing Jacob to feel (verse 23) and smell (verse 27) like his brother. After all, she knows that Isaac is a man who acts on the basis of taste (25:28) and touch (26:8).

The deceit (27:18–29)

As we have seen, Isaac is physically, as well as spiritually, blind (verse 1). Ironically, this double blindness means that the right son, from the point of view of the promise (25:23), is ultimately blessed. But Isaac is not thwarted by his blindness alone, because he can clearly hear that the voice is that of Jacob (verse 22), even though the words deny it (verses 19, 24), and his suspicions are aroused. But he cannot check with any third party; his decision to give the blessing privately, rather than with the whole family present (compare chapter 49), now works against him. Isaac is lethargic. Feeling, tasting and smelling are more significant to him than his hearing. Thus he gives Jacob the blessing appropriate to the firstborn: prosperity (verse 28) and power (verse 29). He has been deceived by 'a combination of smooth words and hairy animals skins' (Janzen, *Abraham and all the Families of the Earth*, page 104).

The agony (27:30–40)

This scene with his father is perhaps the only time we really feel sorry for Esau. The moment at which he realizes that all is lost (verse 34) is a poignant one, however much we feel that he deserves it. But once a blessing is given, there is no back-tracking. Certain words, once spoken, cannot be taken back. In some contexts words do not merely describe a situation, but create a new one: think of the words 'I will' in a wedding ceremony! Words of blessing spoken in God's presence cannot be revoked, even though, of course, it is ultimately God who decides if, and in what way, the words will come true.

Esau knows that his father cannot take back his words – but surely there is still something left? Esau finally does receive a blessing, one more appropriate to his character than the first-born blessing would have been. He is a hunter, and therefore he will live by the sword; he is a loner, and therefore he will live alone (verses 39–40). This echoes the 'blessing' on Ishmael (16:12), once more tying these two characters together.

The flight (27:41 – 28:5)

Rebekah's plan works, but she does not foresee that Esau might want to kill his brother (verse 41). She fears that they might even kill one another (verse 45). As ever, she quickly finds a solution, sending Jacob to her brother, in Haran (verse 43). She promises to send him word when it is safe to return (verse 45). But the message will never be sent: Jacob will remain in Haran for twenty years, and when he returns, it will be to his father alone (35:27).

Rebekah does not tell Isaac the real reason for Jacob's flight, but tells him instead that their son must marry one of the family (verse 46), a theme Isaac repeats in his final blessing on Jacob (verses 1–5). No words of accusation or of repentance are spoken. There is a common understanding that what is done, is done, and perhaps, after all, despite the deceit, it is done for the best.

Questions

1. In the light of verses such as Matthew 12:36, how important do we consider our words to be?

2. In what contexts, and how, might we 'bless' others within our church community?
3. How do you think the quality of family life today compares with that of the families depicted in Genesis?

Genesis 28:10–22

The journey

On our own journeys through life, no matter what our previous mistakes have been, we can be sure of God's presence with us.

Having wrested both the birthright and the blessing from Esau, but now in fear of his life, Jacob begins the next stage of his pilgrimage. Unknown to him, it will also be a highly significant stage in the unfolding of God's promise to make Abraham into a great nation – but that is for the future. For now, he is simply on the run.

Jacob's dream (28:10–17)

Abraham had set out from Haran (12:4) and finally settled in Beersheba (22:19). Jacob now reverses this journey, leaving Beersheba and heading north – passing quickly through Debir, Hebron, Bethlehem and Jerusalem, until he arrives near Bethel, about 53 miles (85 km) from Beersheba – one tenth of his total journey to Haran.

Bethel is the place where his grandfather Abraham built an altar about 160 years before, when he first entered the land (12:8). Here Abraham returned after the Egyptian fiasco (13:3). Here too God told Abraham to look 'north and south, east and west' (13:14), and promised to make Abraham's descendants 'like the dust of the earth' (13:16). It is thus an appropriate location for the Lord to repeat these promises to Abraham's grandson, as he leaves the land, in almost identical words (28:14a), together with the promise that the family will be a blessing to the whole earth (verse 14b; paralleling 12:3).

From a human point of view, in the intervening century and a half, there was little to show: Isaac, and then Jacob, were the only 'chosen' descendants; one burial ground was the only owned land (chapter 23); one local ruler had noticed that God was with them (21:22; 26:28). But at another level much had happened. The sons *had* been born, despite the barrenness of the wives. The rulers *had* noticed that God was with them, despite the failures of the husbands. Land *had* been purchased, despite their status as resident aliens. Lessons in faith and in patience *had* been learned, despite the natural inclination of the family to do things their way rather than God's. The foundations had been carefully laid, even though the house was yet to be built. And a turning point in God's promises was about to be reached: although Jacob was leaving the promised land as a single man, he would return with two wives, eleven sons and a daughter.

The Lord introduces himself to Jacob as 'the God of your father Abraham and the God of Isaac' (verse 13); thus there is continuity between Jacob's experience of God and that of previous generations. But there is also a special promise for Jacob himself, which he will need as he travels into a foreign country: the Lord will be with him, will watch over him, and will bring him back (verse 15). Jacob will always be aware that his stay in Haran is a temporary one, and will have to be careful not to sink deep roots into the area. In a similar way, it is useful for us to remember that we are also 'strangers and exiles' (Hebrews 11:13 RSV) on the earth, and to be encouraged that, during this time, as he was with Jacob, the Lord is also with us (Matthew 28:20).

All of this is placed within the context of a dream of angels ascending and descending a staircase reaching up to God (verse 12). Interpreting dreams is always subjective, but this dream must give Jacob a great sense of both security and awe. Both where he has come from and where he is going are under God's protection (compare Psalm 91:11), and at a place deep within his being there is something reaching up to God, to which God will respond.

As Jacob wakes the next morning, and worships, the world is a different place. It is a much bigger place than he has imagined. He has seen angels, and God has spoken gracious words to him, and will be with him – wherever he goes (verse 15).

Jacob's vow (28:18–22)

In the surrounding culture it was common for large stones to be set up as religious monuments, and Jacob thus converts his stone pillow into a pillar, which he dedicates to God by pouring oil over it. At a later stage in Israel's history such stones will be banned (Deuteronomy 16:21–22; Exodus 23:24); being a feature of Canaanite religion they might too easily lead the people astray. For Jacob, however, this is not a danger, and Jacob responds to God in the way he knows best. In addition, this feat of strength prepares us (and him) for his act of rolling away the stone from the well (29:10).

Jacob vows that if God keeps his side of the promise, 'the LORD will be my God' (verse 21). This is hardly a heroic speech, as there is still much of the old 'bargaining' Jacob here. There is a long way to go, but at least Jacob has begun his spiritual pilgrimage in earnest, and at least he keeps his word.

Abraham gave Melchizedek a tithe (14:20), and Jacob models himself on his grandfather by offering to give the Lord a tenth of all that God gives him (verse 22). In a similar way, although Christians are not under any legalistic obligation to give a set percentage of their income back to God, we certainly ought to model ourselves on those who are generous towards God, such as the Macedonian churches Paul describes (2 Corinthians 8:1–4).

Questions

1. In what ways might God still use dreams to communicate with his people?
2. How can your church encourage its members to be generous in their giving without becoming legalistic or self-righteous?
3. Should the church overseas ban rituals previously used in another religion, or should it seek to incorporate them within a Christian framework?

Poetic justice

God often disciplines us by allowing us to be treated as we have treated others.

After his vision, Jacob buoyantly continues his journey, but he must be nervous as he approaches Haran. Will Laban give this penniless fugitive the same welcome Abraham's servant, with his valuable bride-price, received?

The welcome (29:1–14a)

When Abraham's servant came to find a wife for Isaac, he went to the local well to test which of the local girls would make a suitable partner (24:11). As Jacob comes into the vicinity of Haran, he too approaches a well (verse 2) and begins talking to the local shepherds. The narrator explains the custom there of waiting until all the shepherds have gathered, before the flocks are watered (verses 2–3), presumably to prevent any one shepherd from taking more than their fair share.

Then Rachel appears, and it is love at first sight! Jacob tries to encourage the shepherds to leave quickly (verse 7), but this being impossible (verse 8), he defies custom and performs the heroic feat – emulating his mother's feat of watering ten camels (24:20) – of rolling the large stone away himself, and watering the flock.

Rachel watches, bewildered, as this stranger waters her flock, kisses her, and then begins to weep (verse 11)! Jacob quickly discloses his identity, and Rachel runs to fetch her father Laban, who hurries to meet Jacob (verse 13; compare 24:29).

The weddings (29:14b–30)

Jacob enters Laban's household having proved his strength, rather than as a supplicant on his knees. He has always been a hard worker, and quickly joins Laban's workforce. His wage, for seven years' work, is to be Rachel (verse 18) – for unlike Abraham's servant (24:22, 53) Jacob has no bride-price to give other than his labour.

At the end of seven years there is a rather informal wedding feast, and then, for the first time, Jacob is outwitted. He takes his heavily veiled bride to his room, sleeps with her, and in the morning looks into her eyes (compare verse 17), receiving the greatest shock of his life: for it was Leah (verse 25)! (It is not clear in the Hebrew whether her eyes (verse 17) were her only point of beauty, or whether they detracted from whatever beauty she had; but either way Rachel was the more attractive sister.)

All of this is poetic justice, of course. Had not Jacob himself impersonated his elder brother, deceiving his blind father, in order to gain the blessing? And now the firstborn Leah impersonates her sister, and deceives Jacob – made blind by the darkness, and relying on his sense of touch – in order to gain a husband. Jacob, the younger son, tricked his brother in order to become the firstborn; and he is himself tricked into marrying the firstborn, rather than her younger sister. This is all a part of God's plan for transforming Jacob, the deceiver (27:36; compare Psalm 18:26). Jacob needs to be on the receiving end before he can become the man God wants him to be. Like Esau there is no going back now for Jacob; what is done is done, and he has to make the best of it.

We are never told what Rachel thought about this. Did she ever love Jacob, a man much older than her, as much as he loved her? Did she perhaps agree to her sister impersonating her, in the hope of being free to marry someone else? Perhaps the latter is unlikely – but we do need to remember that Rachel was a deeply ambiguous character. Later she would 'sell' Jacob for some mandrakes (30:15), steal the household gods (31:19) and deceive her father (31:35). We might wonder at times whether her beauty was ever more than skin-deep.

Jacob angrily confronts Laban, who gives a feeble excuse (verses 25–26); but if Jacob is concerned about the rights of the firstborn, he can hardly complain, and Laban now holds the upper hand. He suggests that Jacob marry Rachel as well, at the end of the week, and work for another seven years. Jacob has little choice but to agree (verses 27–30).

The section ends on a tense note. Jacob has come from a family where favouritism ultimately led to the threat of murder, yet he cannot help but have favourites himself: 'He loved Rachel more than Leah' (verse 30). Later he will love Joseph 'more than any of his other sons' (37:3), and this favouritism will almost destroy his own family in turn.

Questions

1. What examples are there in your life when God has disciplined you in a 'poetically just' way?
2. In what ways do we tend to judge people superficially within our church community, ignoring the deeper aspects of their character?
3. How would you answer someone from another culture who claimed that polygamy was biblically acceptable, on the basis of narratives such as this one?

Genesis 29:31 – 30:24

Living with unfulfilled desires

Living with the pain of unfulfilled desires is a common experience. There are times when God finally grants us those desires, but at other times he calls us to endure them – but then he gives us the strength we need.

The conflict between brothers in Genesis is transformed in this section into a conflict between sisters. As Jacob struggled with Esau, so Leah now struggles with Rachel for the heart of Jacob, and for the status of bearing his sons.

Leah gets the upper hand (29:31 – 30:13)

The Lord is God of the poor and marginalized. Thus he comes alongside Leah (verse 31), who is 'not loved', and enables her to bear children. First Reuben is born, then Simeon, then Levi, and then Judah (verses 33–35), and Leah never quite gives up hoping that Jacob will love her. Meanwhile Rachel, Jacob's favourite wife, has to watch, increasingly frustrated as month after month her barrenness continues. She shares the agony of the other patriarchal wives, Sarah and Rebekah, but with no promise to give her hope of a future child.

125

As jealousy of her sister grows, Rachel becomes desperate and blames Jacob (verse 1). Like Esau (25:32), Rachel feels that if her immediate needs are not met she will die. Ironically, she later does give birth to sons; and in giving birth to the second, dies.

She then follows the example of Sarai (16:1–2) by giving her maidservant Bilhah to Jacob as a concubine through whom she can have children. The strategy is 'successful' in that Dan, and then Naphtali, are born, and Rachel claims that God has vindicated her (verse 6) – although we should not necessarily agree with her judgment in this. God does remember her, but not until verse 22. The later history of the tribe of Dan might well suggest that her manipulation of the situation only leads to long-term damage to Israel (see 49:16–18).

Leah, eager to maintain the advantage over her sister, likewise gives *her* maidservant Zilpah to Jacob, and Gad is born, followed by Asher (verses 9–13).

Further schemes (30:14–21)

By now Jacob has stopped sleeping with Leah (verse 15), and Rachel remains barren. Neither sister is likely to bear children in the near future! Into this situation Reuben, Leah's eldest, brings a mandrake plant, which in ancient times was credited with powers of restoring fertility. Rachel, clutching at any straw now, requests some for herself, in return offering Leah Jacob's company for the night. Annoyingly for Rachel, Leah comes out of this scheme better, as she again falls pregnant, this time with Issachar (verses 17–18), while Rachel's barrenness continues.

The narrator completes the family of Leah by noting the births of Zebulun (verse 20) and then a daughter, Dinah (verse 21).

Rachel remembered (30:22–24)

The pain of a marriage without love (as for Leah), or without children (as for Rachel), is a common one, and it is one God understands from the inside. Frequently his own relationship to Israel is described in terms of a marriage, but one in which Israel neither loves him nor bears the fruit for which he longs. There are times when God steps into such situations, and gives people the desires of their hearts; but there are other times when he simply remains in the background, whispering, if we have ears to hear, 'My grace is sufficient for you, for my power is made perfect in weakness' (2 Corinthians 12:9). In the case of Leah, it is unclear whether she ever won the love of her husband – her pain in that area of her life may well have been unending. In the case of Rachel, however, God does 'remember' her (verse 22; compare 8:1): the turning point of the story is reached, for she conceives and gives birth to Joseph. She then prays for a second son (verse 24), a prayer which will be answered, but only at the cost of her life (35:16–20).

In biblical narratives children born after a long period of barrenness often play a significant role in Israel's history. We have already had the examples of Isaac and Jacob; and elsewhere we have the examples of Samson (Judges 13), Samuel (1 Samuel 1) and John the Baptist (Luke 1). Thus it will come as no surprise that the closing quarter of the book of Genesis (chapters 37 – 50) is devoted to the story of Joseph.

Questions

1. To what extent should we seek to fulfil our human desires legitimately, and to what extent should we depend upon God's grace to endure the pain?
2. How can your church act as a support group for those who have to bear the pain of unfulfilled desires in their family life?
3. Scientific techniques are increasingly used to combat infertility. What are the benefits and dangers of these, and at what point might Christians protest that 'enough is enough'?

Genesis 30:25–43

Prosperity out of adversity

There are times when it is right to submit to injustice, and simply to trust God for the outcome.

Laban's deceit (30:25–36)

Jacob has served Laban for seven years after his marriage to Rachel (29:30). He is now free to return to his homeland, and the birth of Joseph seems to have settled his mind in that direction (verse 25). Laban, however, is reluctant to see him go: Jacob is a capable worker, and Laban realizes that his own prosperity is due to the blessing he has received through Jacob being with him (verse 27). He proposes that Jacob continue to work for him, but now as a salaried worker (verse 28). Having been deceived by Laban once (29:25), Jacob is deeply suspicious of Laban's motives, and wants a greater degree of independence. He therefore reminds Laban of all that he has done for him (verses 29–30), and Laban instead offers him a gift (verse 31a). In the same way that Abraham did not want to receive the cave of Machpelah as a gift (23:13), Jacob does not want to receive a gift from Laban, with the social indebtedness that that might imply (verse 31b). He will, however, split the flock between them, and to distinguish between the two flocks he will take those with 'speckled or spotted' coats as his wages (verses 32–33). Laban agrees to this (verse 34) – and immediately removes all such animals from the flocks so that there will be nothing for Jacob to take (verses 35–36).

Jacob's strategy (30:37–43)

Jacob, this time, does not confront Laban in person. Instead he devises a longer-term strategy for ensuring that he will ultimately 'win'. Precisely what he does raises puzzling questions, as there seems to be no genetic reason why flocks mating in front of striped branches should produce spotted or speckled offspring. In his later report to Rachel and Leah (31:7–9), Jacob acknowledges that God has been in control of the process. Laying out the branches may well be an aid to Jacob's faith, an enacted prayer to God both to remember and to bless him, while his careful discrimination between the strong and the weak animals (verses 41–42) and his knowledge of animal husbandry also play their part. Gradually his own share increases, while Laban's share diminishes; and like his grandfather (13:2) and father (26:13) before him he becomes wealthy. The tension between the two men begins to increase.

We should be careful not to be so 'superspiritual' that we despise legitimate aids to our faith, which will often appeal more to the intuitive, symbolic side of our nature than to the rational. As long as we do not regard such actions superstitiously, as if God can be manipulated by them, they can be of great help to us. When Hezekiah receives a threatening letter from Sennacherib, he symbolically spreads it out before the Lord (2 Kings 19:14), and the Lord answers his prayer. Jesus himself often performs symbolic actions which are not strictly necessary for a prayer to be answered; for example putting mud on the eyes of a blind man and telling him to wash in the Pool of Siloam (John 9:6–7). Others know that he could heal simply with a word (for example Matthew 8:8); but in order to build up the faith of the blind man it is helpful for a symbolic action to accompany the word.

We have already noted the negative elements in Jacob's character, but here he appears to get it right! Laban alters his wages ten times (3:1) and Jacob patiently bears the injustice of what is happening, acting as wisely as he knows, and trusting God for the outcome. As the years pass it is clear that God is blessing him. During this time Joseph, in his formative years, is no doubt watching his father – for the qualities shown by Jacob are exactly the ones Joseph will need when he suffers major injustices in his own life.

Questions

1. When should we submit to injustice, and trust God for the outcome; and when should we protest against it?
2. As a church, how can you get the balance right between 'action' and 'prayer'?
3. Jacob's wealth indicated God's blessing upon him, but in the lives of others how can we distinguish whether wealth is in fact a blessing from God or not?

Genesis 31:1–55

A parting of the ways

There are times when it is right to move on. But there are right and wrong ways of doing so.

As with Abraham and Lot (chapter 13), as later with Jacob and Esau (36:7), so now with Laban and Jacob. There comes a time when it is right to separate and to move on.

Jacob's flight (31:1–21)

Guidance is never easy, but in these first few verses events combine to let Jacob know it is time to move on. Laban's attitude has shifted, and his sons are issuing veiled threats against Jacob (verses 1–2). In this context Jacob hears the Lord directing him back to Canaan (verse 3).

Jacob, sure that Laban will try to stop him leaving, devises a plan to flee secretly. His first task is to persuade the rest of the family to agree, so he brings Leah and Rachel out to the fields (verse 4), where they will not be overheard, and reviews the way God has protected him over the years despite the duplicity of Laban (verses 5–9). He also reports to them the dream in which God has told him to return (verses 10–13).

Flight will mean, in effect, being cut out of the family inheritance, but Leah and Rachel agree to this, pointing out that their inheritance has already been used up by their father (verses 14–15). They therefore begin the journey immediately (verses 17–18), heading towards Gilead (verse 21), with just enough time for Rachel to take her father's *teraphim* – small figurines representing the household gods (verse 19).

Clearly, it was right to leave; it is less clear that it was right to leave in this way. The narrator appears to frown upon Jacob's decision (verse 20), placing it on the same level as Rachel's theft. Despite the human threat to Jacob, he has had a specific promise that God will bring him back safely (28:15); and, although obedience to God takes precedence

over human loyalties, it does not justify trampling over legitimate human courtesy (compare Exodus 4:18).

Laban's accusation (31:22–35)

Jacob takes his family and flocks, and it is three days before
Laban hears that they have gone (verse 22). The household gods
have also disappeared, and Laban naturally connects the two
events. He sets off in pursuit and finally overtakes Jacob in
Gilead, east of the Jordan. In the meantime, God has spoken to
Laban, using words Laban himself uttered in 24:50, and has
warned him not to act deceitfully towards Jacob (verses 23–25).

Laban's opening comment (verse 26) echoes 29:25, but his
complaint to Jacob (verses 26–30) is, at best, a half-truth. It is
hard to believe that he would celebrate the departure of Jacob
with 'joy and singing' (verse 27), but he needs to suggest this in
order to make his next accusation more plausible: that Jacob has
fled because he has stolen the household gods (verse 30).

Jacob admits his fear of Laban, but naturally denies taking the
gods. Not knowing that Rachel has taken them, he then gives
Laban the power to search his camp (verses 31–32), with a rash
oath that he might have lived to regret (as did Jephthah in
Judges 11:29–40). The search is fruitless, as Rachel has no
hesitation in deceiving her father (verses 33–35). Surely Laban
will not suspect her of bringing sacred objects into close contact
with her impurity? Thus Laban, the deceiver, is himself
deceived.

Laban and Jacob's treaty (31:36–55)

Jacob is now sufficiently angry to confront Laban, and publicly
accuses him of wishing him harm (verses 36–42). Laban retal-
iates by suggesting that all Jacob's possessions actually belong
to him, but that he can do nothing now that Jacob has fled with
them (verse 43). Before Jacob can respond further, however,
Laban suggests that they make a covenant, symbolized by a
heap of stones and a pillar (compare 28:18), to preserve the
peace between them, and this they do, in the name of the God of
their ancestors (verses 45–54). 'Early the next morning' Laban
returns home (verse 55).

Jacob has now made peace with Laban, but still has to face
Esau, who twenty years earlier had threatened to kill him (27:41).
How would he react to seeing his younger brother returning?

Questions

---

1. How do we know when it is right to move on, rather than simply 'escape' from difficulties that God would prefer us to face?
2. To what extent should your church community be involved in the major decisions that you have to make in life?
3. What are the advantages and disadvantages of living in a mobile society with few roots?

Genesis 32:1–32

Preparing for the showdown

In facing a situation of danger, it is wise to prepare well – and to pray!

As Jacob re-enters the land, he is dominated by the fear that Esau still wishes to kill him. Twenty years have passed, but has the anger passed from Esau's heart?

Mahanaim (32:1–2)

When Jacob left the promised land he had a vision of angels at Bethel; now, as he approaches Canaan, he is once more met by angels. He has reached Mahanaim, probably on the northern bank of the river Jabbok, which is where David later flees from Absalom (2 Samuel 17:24). The name means 'two camps', referring both to Jacob's own camp and 'the camp of God' (verse 2). By this means Jacob is reassured that God has not forgotten his promise to be with him, and to bring him back safely (28:15).

Jacob's message (32:3–6)

Wisely, Jacob then sends word that he is coming. This would give Esau time to respond graciously, but it would also give him time to prepare an armed force! In fairness, Esau is probably as unsure of Jacob's motives as Jacob is of his. But the sight of 400 men (verse 6; compare 14:14) on the march northwards does nothing to dispel Jacob's anxiety.

Jacob's prayer (32:7–12)

Jacob responds to the apparent threat in two ways. Practically, he seeks to minimize the damage, should Esau attack, by dividing his possessions into two groups (verses 7–8); and then he prays the most agonized prayer of his life – under the circumstances quite a model prayer! He addresses God as the God of Abraham and Isaac, implicitly reminding God of his covenant with Abraham and with his descendants. He states that God has commanded him to make this journey (verse 9; compare 31:3) and reminds him also of all that God has done for him (verse 10). He confesses his fear and prays for God to rescue him (verse 11), appealing to him on the basis of his longer-term promises to the family (verse 12; compare 28:14).

This is a good model to follow should we ever need to pray such a prayer. We cannot always appeal to God on the basis of such direct promises, but we *can* always know that he will be with us (Matthew 28:20), and we can be reminded that no matter what the external circumstances, nothing can separate us from Christ's love (Romans 8:35).

Jacob's gift (32:13–21)

In addition, Jacob also tries appeasement. He hopes to wear away Esau's anger by one gift after another: 'A soft answer turns away wrath', the writer of Proverbs (15:1 RSV) reminds us. Jacob's answer is as soft as the fleece of 200 sheep and over 350 other assorted animals (verses 13–15)! And then all he can do is wait (verse 21).

Jacob at the Jabbok (32:22–32)

Jacob sends his possessions on ahead, and decides to spend the night alone. He is preparing to meet Esau, in what he thinks will be the most dramatic encounter of his life; but instead he meets God.

Whereas at the beginning of the chapter Jacob has been met by the angels of God (verses 1–2), now, in one of the most

133

mysterious, baffling and awe-inspiring passages of the entire book, a man appears who 'wrestled with him till daybreak' (verse 24). There is a sense in which Jacob has been wrestling all his life: with his brother, with Laban, with his father, with himself, but most of all, underlying all the others, with God. And this night is the climax of his spiritual pilgrimage. At the deepest roots of his being, from the time of his birth and reflected in his name, which he is forced to acknowledge (verse 27), he is 'the grasper'. Now, no longer hiding behind deceit or diplomacy, he grasps hold of God and will not let him go until he has been blessed (verse 26). This is why God has made him a grappler: not to grasp the rights of an Esau, or the possessions of a Laban, but to lay hold of God, to grasp what only God can give him. Jacob now knows this and will not let go. Whether he lives or dies, the only thing of importance is to embrace, and to be embraced by, God.

At Bethel Jacob learned he was in the house of God (28:17); now he learns what it means to be in God's grip, and he expects to die (compare verse 30). But instead he is blessed (verse 29) and, as a result of his all-night labour, a new identity is brought to birth: 'Israel', 'he struggles with God' (verses 28). He discovers that being 'Jacob', the trickster, is not the most important thing; deeper down he is an 'Israel'. In contrast to the setting sun at Bethel (28:11), the sun now rises (verse 31), and Jacob/Israel returns in the early morning light, triumphantly limping. Even the wounds we receive from God are holy.

Questions

1. In what areas of your life might you be wrestling with God?
2. In what ways could your church give space for people to acknowledge poor relationships and allow them the opportunity for healing them?
3. When might 'a soft answer' be appropriate in international politics, or will it always be interpreted negatively as 'appeasement'?

Christians are called to be reconciled to one another and to be peacemakers between others, thus demonstrating the heart of God to the world.

 Jacob has been reconciled to Laban, and to God. But Esau has threatened to take Jacob's life (27:41); and Esau is travelling towards him with four hundred men (32:6; 33:1). Will this be a third reconciliation, or a bloodbath?

Beyond all expectation (33:1–7)

Jacob divides up his family (verses 1–2). He gives the greatest honour, and the best chance of avoiding injury, to Rachel and Joseph, and leaves the maidservants and their children in the position of greatest vulnerability. He then approaches his brother alone and gives him great honour, in the hope of appeasing any anger that Esau might still feel (verse 3). Esau's reaction is more than Jacob can have hoped for. Like the father in Jesus' parable of the prodigal son (Luke 15:20) Esau runs and embraces the younger brother (verse 4). Jacob then introduces his family (verses 5–7).

Implicit forgiveness (33:8–11)

Jacob has sent on ahead more than five hundred animals as a gift to Esau (32:13–21). It is a small recompense for what he has earlier stolen from his brother (27:36) – indeed, he calls it a 'blessing' (verse 11; NIV: 'present'), symbolically returning the blessing he had stolen (chapter 27). Jacob is content now with the blessing he has received from God (32:29). Esau's acceptance of the gift (verse 11) implies that he is now willing to drop his vendetta against his brother (27:41).

Neither brother refers explicitly to the events of the past, although those events loom large in the background of the story and in their minds. What is done cannot be undone, and what has been said cannot be taken back. Esau now wants to resume normal relationships, and although Jacob refers diplomatically to Esau as 'my lord' (verse 8), to Esau, Jacob is simply, and quite genuinely, 'my brother' (verse 9).

Esau's words dissolve the fear that has hung over Jacob for twenty years. The previous night Jacob has, as it were, looked God in the face for the first time (32:30), and now he can do the same to Esau: it is 'like seeing the face of God' all over again (verse 10; compare Psalm 133:1).

Christians, too, are called by Jesus to be 'reconciled to your brother' (Matthew 5:24), and Paul reminds the Colossians to 'forgive whatever grievances you may have against one another. Forgive as the Lord forgave you' (Colossians 3:13). It is somewhat ironic that we learn this lesson from Esau, who is usually such a negative example (for example Hebrews 12:16)!

Lingering suspicion (33:12–20)

Jacob and Esau have publicly made up their differences, but Jacob still has lingering suspicions about his brother's motivation. Esau offers to accompany Jacob home, but Jacob quickly finds an excuse why it is better for Esau to go on ahead (verses 12–14). The excuse is feeble, for Esau must know as well as Jacob the speed that the flocks can move at. In any case he has to move hundreds of his own livestock, the gift from Jacob, at the same time. But Jacob, having achieved the reconciliation he desires, now wants to be separated from his brother as quickly as possible. Esau then offers to leave some of his men to help Jacob, but Jacob counters this by arguing that the only thing he wants from Esau is Esau's favour (verse 15).

Finally Esau returns to his homeland. Jacob says that he will travel slowly 'until I come to my lord in Seir' (verse 14), which is south of the Dead Sea. In fact, Jacob does nothing of the sort. He establishes a base nearby at Succoth, near to the river Jabbok, and then heads west to the city of Shechem (verse 18). He has little intention of moving any further.

Shechem was the first resting place of Abraham, Jacob's grandfather, when he also travelled south from Haran about 180 years before (12:6), and, like Abraham (12:7), Jacob builds an altar there (verse 20). Following Abraham's example he also buys land from the local inhabitants (verse 19), although we have none of the protracted negotiations of chapter 23. This plot of land later becomes significant as the place where Joseph's bones are buried after the exodus from Egypt (Joshua 24:32).

Jacob has been reconciled three times over, but why, with the whole land to choose from, does he pitch his tents near Shechem (verses 18–19)? Is he fulfilling the promise made to Abraham at Shechem 'To your offspring I will give this land' (12:7)? Or is there instead an echo of Lot, who 'pitched his tents near Sodom' (13:12)?

Questions

1. If there are any people with whom you need to be reconciled, pray now for wisdom and courage to make the first move towards peace.
2. Churches have often been split by personal grudges. How can your church develop a spirituality that prevents such vendettas from growing?
3. How can Christians be more effectively involved in being peacemakers in the world?

Genesis 34:1–31

Responding to sexual violation

When a person is the victim of sexual abuse, how should we deal with the attacker?

At the end of the last study we questioned the wisdom of settling so close to Shechem. Years have gone by, however, with no ill-effects, and the children are now much older. Jacob is so confident of the safety of the area that he permits his daughter to go out without protection, until one day the unthinkable happens, and his only daughter is sexually violated. How should he respond to this crisis?

The act (34:1–12)

Shechem is the name of the city, but it is also the name of the son of that city's ruler, Hamor. No doubt Shechem has exploited his family connections and is quite used to getting his own way. He sees Dinah visiting the women of the land (verse 1), and without further thought or scruple he sexually violates her (verse 2).

Shechem is drawn towards Dinah and desires to marry her, although the way he expresses this to his father is insultingly abrupt (verses 3–4). Nevertheless, he appears quite serious about his plan, and in order to accomplish it is later willing to pay whatever bride-price is demanded from him (verse 12), and to endure circumcision (verse 19).

Rape is an appalling crime, but it may be that 'rape' (NIV) is too strong a translation of the Hebrew word in verse 2, the same word used, for example, when Jacob 'slept with' Leah (30:16). Only the context can help us decide the nature of the act, and in the context of Shechem and Dinah it might be that 'seduction', rather than 'rape', is a more appropriate description. The narrator gives no account of any violent struggle (compare 2 Samuel 13:12–14), and Shechem's later actions are hardly typical of a rapist, in contrast to Amnon (2 Samuel 13:15–17). Dinah even remains in his house (verse 26). In seducing Dinah Shechem has abused his position of power, but his sin seems to have brought him somewhat to his senses. Incidentally, if Shechem had been an Israelite living under the Mosaic legislation, he would automatically have *had* to marry Dinah (Deuteronomy 22:28–29). Under other circumstances this young man, 'the most honoured of all his father's household' (verse 19), might yet have become an honourable ruler after his father.

The fathers, Hamor and Jacob, wish to draw a veil over the whole affair (verses 5–6). Shechem's appeal to 'find favour' in the eyes of Jacob (verse 11) must have touched the heart of a man who, not long before, had also desperately needed to 'find favour' in the eyes of someone he had sinned against (33:8, 15). If it had been left to them, Shechem and Dinah would soon have married – although one wonders what Jacob's reaction would have been if Dinah had been Rachel's daughter rather than Leah's (verse 1).

But, for better or for worse, it is not left for the fathers to decide.

The deceit (34:13–24)

Dinah's brothers quickly take over the negotiations from their father, and from this point on Jacob is dominated by his sons, as he withdraws into a more reflective mood (verses 5; 35:22; 37:11). They demand that the Shechemites be circumcised – only this will permit the intermarriage that the Shechemites demand (verses 13–17). Hamor and Shechem agree (verse 18), but then have to persuade the rest of their townspeople that this will be in their best interests. This they do in a highly political speech (verses 20–23), using slogans such as 'one people' (verse 22) which they have picked up from Dinah's brothers (verse 16), and emphasizing the economic advantages that will accrue to them (verse 23). The speech is followed by the knife, and all the males are circumcised (verse 24).

The vengeance (34:25–31)

We are not told why the brothers wait three days. Are the Shechemites weakest at this time? Or are the brothers having second thoughts, debating whether to go ahead with their plan? In the end, despite the initial anger of them all, only Simeon and Levi (who have a reputation for hot-headed violence, 49:5–7) put the plan into action (verse 25). The massacre is complete, Dinah is 'rescued' (verses 25–26), and the rest of the brothers join in looting the city (verses 27–29).

Jacob, naturally, is fearful for the future of his family; it is obvious that he will be outnumbered if the local towns make an alliance against him. Soon afterwards he is no doubt glad to hear the voice of God calling him to move on, albeit only to Bethel, 20 miles south of Shechem (35:1).

Simeon and Levi defend their actions (verse 31), for clearly Shechem has sinned grievously against their sister. But their revenge goes far beyond even the later Mosaic principle of 'an eye for an eye' (Exodus 21:23–25), and many innocent people lose their lives. Society needs a system of law and order, but if we are ever in a position of acting as God's disciplinary instrument in the life of another, we need to be sure that we are not substituting our own agenda for the Lord's. God's people are called to leave vengeance to God (Deuteronomy 32:35; quoted in Romans 12:19; Hebrews 10:30; compare Matthew 26:52).

Questions

---

1. How can we ensure that we are not being influenced by our own interests when we are responsible for disciplining someone else?
2. How can your church provide a safe haven for those who have been sexually abused to work through their emotions?
3. How can we balance the need for society to punish the guilty, with the demand for God's people not to take personal vengeance?

Genesis 35:1–15

Roots

Sometimes it is good to go back to the place where God first called us, to recommit ourselves and to hear his voice once more.

It would be hard for Jacob to remain near Shechem after the events of chapter 34. We learn later in this chapter that his father Isaac is still alive, and has moved north from Beersheba (26:23) to Mamre, near Hebron  (35:27), where Abraham also stayed (13:18). Jacob decides to move south, ultimately to join his father; but the road south passes through Bethel, where he had had his initial vision of the angels ascending and descending a ladder (28:10–22). God's initial command to him is to return as far as Bethel, and there to build an altar (35:1).

Back to Bethel (35:1–7)

When Abraham came into the land, he built an altar at Bethel (12:8), and returned there after the events in Egypt in an act of recommitment (13:3) before going down to Hebron (13:18). There is now a similar sequence in the life of Jacob. Having received his initial vision of God at Bethel (28:10–22), he also now recommits himself at Bethel after the events in Haran and in Shechem, before he too moves south to Hebron (35:27).

It is good for us sometimes to 'revisit' places (whether literally or in our imagination) where we have received a special promise or commissioning from God, where we have made a special commitment to God, or where he has acted in a special way in the life of our family, community or nation. It reminds us of what he has done for us, and strengthens us to face the future, and it may also provide the right context for us to hear God's voice again.

The recommitment for Jacob involved, first, getting rid of anything hindering his relationship with God. Rachel, we know, had earlier stolen the household gods (31:19), but many others within this now sizeable community probably also have their idols with them. Jacob symbolically buries these idolatrous objects before departing (verse 4); 'earrings' are mentioned as these were often fashioned in the form of figurines representing deities. He then instructs the family to 'change their clothes' (verse 2) as a symbol of the new start they are making. Jacob's fear of an attack (34:30) never materializes, as 'the terror of God' falls on the towns around them (verse 5; compare Exodus 15:13–18; Joshua 2:9), and they arrive safely at Bethel, where Jacob fulfils his commission and builds an altar to God (verse 7).

Confirming the covenant (35:8–15)

We learn in verse 8 that 'Deborah, Rebekah's nurse', has been with Jacob's household. She must have been a deeply significant figure in Jacob's troubled upbringing, perhaps giving him some of the security he desperately needed. It may have been that she had come to inform Jacob when his mother Rebekah had died, and had remained with him since then. Deborah herself now dies, and is honoured by being buried under a distinctive tree near the town (verse 8).

Now God speaks to Jacob again, and blesses him (verse 9). In a sense, there is nothing new in what God says, but there is a difference in the hearer, for he is no longer 'Jacob', but 'Israel' (verse 10). God confirms the promises he had made to the patriarchal family, promises Jacob may first have heard from the lips of his grandfather Abraham (for Jacob was fifteen when Abraham died), and then from the lips of his father Isaac, and then for himself, at Bethel, on the way to Haran (28:13–15). Now, as he returns to Bethel, an older and wiser man, the refrain continues, and once more the familiar words give direction to his life.

This, too, is a consolation to us. God does not always speak 'life-changing' words to us: sometimes his words are consoling, or encouraging; at other times they may be no different from what we have heard before, but we need to hear them again, because we are human, and deep down we are children needing to hear the same story read once more.

One new line, however, echoes not the promise to Abraham, but the blessing upon Adam (1:28) and Noah (9:1): 'be fruitful and increase in number' (verse 11). No longer will there simply be a chosen line; it is the right time for God's purposes to move onwards, so that there will soon be a chosen people, whose calling will be to demonstrate to the surrounding nations God's original relationship with humanity. We, too, are inheritors of that commission.

Jacob responds, simply, as before. Once more he sets up a pillar, pours oil upon it (verse 14; compare 28:18), and names the place 'Bethel' (verse 15; compare 28:19), because once more God has spoken to him.

Questions

1. What places in your life might you name 'Bethel' – where God has spoken to you?
2. In what ways might your church symbolize a new beginning, leaving the past behind?
3. In what ways does the worldwide church demonstrate the relationship with God that he originally intended to have with the whole of humanity?

Genesis 35:16 – 37:1

Two families and two funerals

God brings certain things to completion before moving on to the next stage in his purposes, but what he completes may itself be the springboard launching that next stage.

 This is perhaps not a good passage for a group discussion! Nevertheless, it has an important function in the overall flow of the book, setting the scene for the story of Joseph to follow. Benjamin, Joseph's younger brother, is born, and Rachel, Joseph's mother, dies, as does Isaac. The story of Esau's family is then summarized, clearing the ground before the narrator launches us fully into the career of Joseph.

The death of Rachel (35:16–20)

Eleven sons have been born to Jacob in the 'competition' between his wives in chapters 29 – 30. More years have passed, and Rachel's wish for another son (30:24) is granted – but at the cost of her life (verses 16–18).

Rachel's tomb, overlooking the road between Jerusalem and Bethlehem, was a well-known landmark for the Israelites (see, for example, 1 Samuel 10:2). Centuries later, when the people of Israel are gathering along that same road, at Ramah, to go into exile (Jeremiah 40:1), Jeremiah imagines Rachel watching from her tomb, and 'weeping for her children ... because her children are no more' (Jeremiah 31:15). And centuries later still, Matthew repeats this picture, as the mothers around Bethlehem weep for their children butchered by Herod's soldiers (Matthew 2:16–18).

Reuben's attempted coup (35:21–22a)

The little verse about Reuben (verse 22a) is more important than it seems. Reuben is the firstborn (29:32), and should have had the headship over the family when Jacob dies. But he is aware, as they all are, of Jacob's coolness towards Leah's sons, and he may feel that he will not receive his rights. Thus what is his by right, he tries to take by force – sleeping with his father's concubine is not an act of lust, but a bid for power (compare Absalom in 2 Samuel 16:21–22). Like many of Reuben's plans (compare 37:21; 42:37), this ends in failure: Jacob never forgets the insult, and Reuben loses even what is his by right (49:3–4). Simeon and Levi, by their violence (chapter 34), are also disqualified from receiving the blessing of the firstborn, and thus the fourth-born son, Judah, later assumes the leadership (49:8–12).

The death of Isaac (35:22b–29)

After a summary list of Jacob's sons (verses 22a–26), we are told that Jacob goes home to his father, the first time they have met since Jacob had to flee. Isaac gave his final blessing to Jacob on that occasion (28:1–5), so there is no need to repeat it, although Isaac is now on his deathbed. After his death – as so often at funerals – the brothers put aside their differences (for a time) and together bury their father (compare 25:9).

The migration of Esau (36:1–8)

The descendants of Esau took over the mountainous area south of the Dead Sea and formed the nation of Edom, which was to be a perpetual thorn in the flesh for Israel. However, Edom also had a reputation for wisdom: for example the book of Job is set in Edom (compare Job 1:1 with Lamentations 4:21; see also Jeremiah 49:7), and Esau acts with wisdom here, choosing to migrate away from Jacob in order to avoid conflict when it becomes clear that the land cannot support them both (verse 7; compare 13:6), and also perhaps recognizing that the 'promised' land rightfully belongs to Jacob's descendants (compare 37:1).

The family of Esau (36:9–43)

This complex genealogy begins with a list of Esau's sons (verses 10–14), moves into a list of tribal chiefs in Edom (verses 15–30), and concludes with a list of Edomite kings (verses 31–39). It is difficult to say why the Israelite author includes such a complete record from a nation regarded as an enemy, but it may function as a warning to Israel not to become like their 'brother' nation.

Israel also passed through the stages of being a family, a number of tribes and a monarchy.

The length of the list may have been determined by the number seventy. There are seventy nations listed in Genesis 10, and seventy of Jacob's family are later listed as entering Egypt (Genesis 46:27); so here too seventy different names are listed, which would have given the original readers a sense of 'completeness'. It also demonstrates that even the unchosen line lived, to some degree, under the blessing of God (compare 27:39–40).

Questions

1. What sort of things might we seek to grasp from God that in reality he is willing to give us freely?
2. In the same way that the Israelites drew on the memory of Rachel watching over her children, what traditions might your Christian community draw on to help gain perspective in situations of pain or oppression?
3. What good qualities can you recognize in nations or people groups that are hostile to your own people?

THE STORY OF JOSEPH

JOSEPH

Genesis 37 – 50

Stop and look

As we read through Genesis the individual 'stories' gradually become longer. The cycle of stories about Abraham is made up of lots of individual narratives with few connecting links. Jacob's story is a sequence of connected scenes, and, although there is an over-arching plot, it tends to get lost in the various subplots that keep cropping up. The story of Joseph is undeniably a unity, however. Because of this the author has not needed to impose a unifying structure on to the different elements, as in the previous two cycles. It has a natural rhythm that unrelentingly carries the reader along.

In the popular imagination Joseph is best known for his dreams, and for his 'amazing technicolour dreamcoat'! Both are important themes within the story. The 'richly ornamented robe' (37:3), a sign of his father's favouritism, is stripped from him by his brothers (37:23), only to be replaced later with 'robes of fine linen' (41:42) from Pharaoh. And there are three 'pairs' of dreams, all of which have some bearing on the future: Joseph's two dreams (37:5–11); the dreams of the cupbearer and baker (chapter 40), and Pharaoh's two dreams (41:1–7).

But the story, at its heart, is more than this; it is about God, and about one way in which God fulfils his purposes in human history, and perhaps also in our own history. In the story of Jacob the Lord appeared to take a step backwards, so as to be less prominent than in the life of Abraham. This process continues even more in Joseph's life. Although God still speaks to Jacob in a vision (46:2–4), he never speaks directly to Joseph – even in his dreams he hears no voice. Joseph is flung into a situation where he suffers multiple injustice, but God is silent. Joseph is given a place of honour, but God is still silent. Joseph has to hang on, in faith that God is there, with only the rather ambiguous testimony of his circumstances to back up that claim. No heavenly voice encourages him and no angels comfort him.

In comparison, for example with Jacob, it is less easy to warm to Joseph as a person – he is somewhat obnoxious as an adolescent, a bit too good the rest of the time, and a bit too 'know it all' throughout his life. (This despite his emotional outbursts: eight times he is described as weeping.) Nevertheless his situation is the more common one: people suffer injustice, or receive unexpected 'good fortune', and God is frequently silent. At times,

God simply watches, and allows people (even his saints) to work out for themselves what they should be doing in life, and how the different pieces fit together. As a poster once put it, 'There are no short cuts through the forest of life.' It is only at the end of a long process of battling with his emotions and seeing that somehow things have worked out well, that Joseph can forgive those who have caused him pain and say to them, 'You intended to harm me, but God intended it for good ... ' (50:20).

We would, of course, be abusing this insight if we were to use it to condone injustice or to relax our efforts in the fight against oppression. God may mysteriously use injustice and oppression as his instruments, but nevertheless the calling of the church is to denounce them prophetically. We will never derail God's plans by speaking against evil.

This is the paradox of this story: in comparison with the stories of Abraham and Isaac, God is apparently least involved with Joseph, but at a deeper level he is the most involved. From an external viewpoint God speaks the least, but instead he is communicating what he has to say through the internal dynamics of Joseph's life. Whereas God intervened to prevent harm coming to Isaac (22:12), and prevented Laban harming Jacob (31:29), he does nothing to prevent the brothers harming Joseph, or to prevent unjust accusations being made against him. He thus gives far greater rein to the powers of sin and evil, to the forces of jealousy, anger, pride and lust. He deliberately allows his purposes to be hanging by the slenderest possible thread – and only then does he act: Pharaoh has a dream and those purposes are gradually brought to their fulfilment.

Esther, too, understood this paradox. A Jewess in a foreign country, caught in the harem of a pagan king, with her people (as so often since) under the threat of genocide, with God apparently absent; she too hears no heavenly voice directing her, only the voice of Mordecai asking her to put her life on the line: 'who knows but that you have come to royal position for such a time as this?' (Esther 4:14). And again, as she does so, God acts, and gives the king a sleepless night, and God's purposes once more finally come to fruition.

This is surely the world that we live in, although, as yet, we do not see the final act of God's drama. God's purposes seem to hang by a slender thread at times, with the darkness often seeming to gain the high ground. Nevertheless we can have confidence that even the darkness can serve the purposes of God, because this is the pattern of our faith and, in Christ, we have seen the world from the perspective of the cross.

It is this paradox, in which God is often most involved when he appears most remote, that gives the story of Joseph its resonance with the story of Christ, and perhaps with the stories of our own lives. The near-sacrifice of Isaac (chapter 22) foreshadows something of the cross, but that is merely one incident in Isaac's life. Joseph (unknowingly) has to live an entire life shaped by patterns that bear the fingerprint of God. 'Humiliation' followed by 'exaltation' is a sequence Isaiah later adopts for his description of God's ideal servant (52:13–15), and that Paul uses as the basic pattern of the incarnation and exaltation of Christ (Philippians 2:6–11). The way that God 'meekly' allows evil to do its worst, before bringing his own purposes to a triumphant conclusion, is reflected most clearly in the cross – in the moment when God himself appears to be absent (Matthew 27:46), Christ's decisive victory is won. Joseph's constant need for faith in a God 'who gives life to the dead and calls things that are not as though they were' (Romans 4:17) brings us full circle back to Abraham, and even to the creation itself, as well as reminding us all that Good Friday is followed by Easter Sunday.

Genesis 37:2–36

Sowing the wind, reaping the whirlwind

God often works in hidden ways. Sometimes he even uses sin and evil as instruments to discipline his people and to refine their characters.

Jacob had to grow up in a family where he was not his father's favourite son, and this deeply affected the course of his life. Joseph has the opposite problem: he is the favourite son, but this likewise leads to conflict with his brothers and the threat of death.

The dreamer (37:2–11)

There is no point in pretending that Joseph is an attractive character. He tells tales about his brothers (verse 2) and boasts about the dreams he has had, naïvely imagining that others will find them as fascinating as he does (verses 5–11). It is true that one day Joseph would be a great man of God – but it would need years of suffering and hardship before he would be ready for the task God has laid upon him.

Much of the fault for the tension between the brothers lies with Jacob, who makes it obvious that Joseph, the firstborn son of Rachel, is the apple of his eye. He gives Joseph a 'richly ornamented robe' (verse 3), which makes the situation worse. He then gives Joseph the soft option of being the messenger boy between his brothers and his father (verse 13), rather than tending the flock (verse 2). But this gives his brothers the opportunity they have been waiting for.

The victim (37:12–24)

In order to get good pasturage the brothers have moved Jacob's flocks from the valley of Hebron back to the vicinity of Shechem, an area they know well (33:18–19). Jacob appears blissfully unaware of the potential danger as he sends Joseph on this 100 mile round trip to see how they are. At Shechem Joseph meets a somewhat mysterious (angelic?) figure, who sends him on, another 15 miles or so, to Dothan (verses 15–17). His brothers probably recognize the 'richly ornamented robe' (verse 23) as soon as it appears on the horizon, and they wonder how they might kill their brother (verses 18–20).

Reuben, though, at least thinks about their father (verse 22), although he also has his own agenda. He has incurred the wrath of Jacob by sleeping with Bilhah (35:22), and perhaps sees an opportunity for getting back in his father's good books. He agrees to place Joseph in a cistern, but alive rather than dead, in the hope of rescuing him later (verse 22; compare verse 20).

The slave (37:25–36)

As they eat their meal another opportunity suddenly presents itself. Dothan was very near the Via Maris, the 'Way of the Sea', a trade route that crossed the plain of Jezreel and moved down the coast towards Egypt. A caravan of Midianites (a smaller group within the wider Ishmaelite clans; compare Judges 8:22–24) passes, and the brothers realize that by selling Joseph as a slave they can not only get rid of him, while avoiding the guilt of shedding his blood, but can also receive twenty pieces of silver – two each – into the bargain. This they do (verses 25–28), but unknowingly, and ironically, they set into motion a train of events that will lead directly to the fulfilment of Joseph's dreams.

This is a huge blow for Reuben (verses 29–30), but the more complex problem is what to say to Jacob. Their solution is also ironic. Jacob fooled his own father by slaughtering a goat and presenting himself in the clothing of his brother (chapter 27). Now his sons slaughter a goat and present their brother's blood-stained robe to Jacob, leaving him to draw his own conclusions (verses 31–33). Having fooled his own father, Jacob is now deceived by his sons, and truly believes that Joseph is dead.

Jacob's heart is broken, and he 'refused to be comforted' (verse 35; compare Jeremiah 31:15); his child is no more, and there is nothing left for him to live for.

Unknown to Jacob, a couple of hundred miles away the son for whom he weeps has been sold into the household of Potiphar, an important Egyptian official (verse 36). So near, and yet so far, it will be more than twenty years before they meet again.

Questions

1. In what ways has God brought good out of evil in your own experience of life?
2. How can your church help those going through adolescence to grow in maturity while keeping hold of their dreams?
3. In what ways might God discipline the nations with his 'poetic justice', as in Obadiah 15?

Genesis 38:1–30

Backsliding and restoration

Even when his people drift away from him, God desires to restore their relationship with him – although he may use unusual methods to do so!

 Joseph is in Egypt. The narrator switches our attention to Judah, whose descendants will later play the key role in Israel's history. But Judah has just sold his younger brother into slavery, and now wants nothing more to do with God; so how does God change him into the man who acts with wisdom and responsibility in chapter 43?

Judah's family (38:1–11)

We are not told why Judah leaves home (verse 1). Perhaps he is ashamed of his part in getting rid of Joseph, and cannot face seeing Jacob's grief every day; so he flees, turning his back on God, and looks for a new start. He marries a local Canaanite girl who bears him three sons (verses 3–5). Like any parent, Judah is proud of his sons, and keen to see them settle down. He arranges a marriage for his firstborn; but then reality breaks in, and Er ends up dead (verses 6–7). God has struck his first blow against Judah's defences. Then Onan, the irresponsible second son, dies, being unwilling to father a child on behalf of his brother (verses 8–10). Judah *ought* then to give Tamar in marriage to Shelah, his third son; instead he sends her back to her father (verse 11), and tries to forget her.

Judah had suggested selling Joseph into slavery (37:26), so that his father thought that Joseph was dead (37:33–34), and now Judah is learning what that cost his father, as he experiences his own grief, twice over. He cannot bear to see another son die, and much later will do all that he can to ensure that his father will not have to bear that sorrow either (for example 44:34). God is beginning to transform Judah, but there is a long way to go.

Tamar seeks justice (38:12–23)

Tamar is the rather unlikely instrument God uses to bring Judah to his senses. She does not have a voice in society, but she does have a woman's body. And, like God, she also has patience. She patiently endures being sent back to her father; she waits until Judah's wife has died (verse 12); she waits until shearing time, a time of festivity (compare 1 Samuel 25:7–8); she waits, disguised as a prostitute, for Judah to walk along the road, and then springs her trap (verses 13–14). Soon she has Judah's seal and staff – and his seed within her (verses 15–19). Then she disappears (verses 20–22) and Judah cannot enquire further for fear of being made a laughing stock (verse 23) – for who would give his credit cards to a prostitute?

It is always easy to criticize victims of injustice like Tamar when they act unethically in order to gain a hearing. But from his position of power, Judah deliberately uses the social structures of his day to cover his own hypocrisy and guilt. Jacob had deceived his father (chapter 27), and was in turn deceived into sleeping with a woman disguised as her sister (29:23). Now Judah, having deceived Jacob, *his* father (37:32), is also deceived into sleeping with a woman in disguise!

Judah's guilt and Tamar's twins (38:24–30)

When Judah hears of Tamar's pregnancy (verse 24) he sees his chance to get rid of an unwanted responsibility and start again with a new wife for Shelah. He gives his instant judgment (verse 24b): 'Burn her to death!' Judah is not the first man, nor the last, to express this double standard (see Hosea 4:14; and where is the guilty *man* in John 8:3?).

Tamar returns Judah's possessions and casually asks whether he recognizes them (verse 25), echoing the moment that Judah, with his brothers, sent Joseph's bloodstained robe to their father and asked whether he recognized it (37:32). Judah realizes that he is caught in a trap not only of his own making, or of Tamar's making, but ultimately a trap of God's making. His hypocrisy has caught up with him, and his double guilt is now public knowledge. Instead of defending himself, however, he finally acknowledges (verse 26), 'She is more righteous than I', and that confession makes all the difference.

Judah can now continue his pilgrimage with God. When we meet him again, he will be a wiser, more chastened figure. In the meantime, although repentance brings a person back to God, it cannot turn the clock back. Two of Judah's sons have died after marrying Tamar, and now, through Tamar, two more sons are born to him (verse 27). The delivery is difficult: one baby puts out a hand, but the other is born first (verses 28–30). This painful twist at the end of the story tells us that God has not given up on this family, for all its failings – he is still choosing the younger brother. Perez, not Zerah, will be named in the genealogy of David (Ruth 4:18–22), and Jesus (Matthew 1:3).

Questions

1. If there is anyone whom you are not treating with justice, think about what you can do to correct the situation.
2. In what ways can your church practically express its concern for people who are victims of injustice in your own locality?
3. Many people throughout the world suffer injustice. What can you do to 'Speak up for those who cannot speak for themselves' (Proverbs 31:8)?

Levirate marriage

It may seem strange that Tamar expected to be married to the brother of her dead husband, but there were good reasons for this social custom. In all ancient societies it was normal for women to be kept within their father's home until they were married (usually in their early teens). They were then 'protected' by their husband. But what happened if their husband died? And if there were no children, would not the family name of the husband die out? And would the woman not be left in a vulnerable position? If they remarried, who would receive the inheritance of the land?

To help prevent these problems many societies evolved variations on a system that has been called 'levirate marriage'. The basic instructions for Israel are given by Moses in Deuteronomy 25:5–10, although this reflects a much older custom. The basic principle is that if a married man died without an heir, a younger brother would marry the widow, and for legal purposes their first

155

son would be regarded as the child of the dead brother. There are many details we are ignorant of, such as, what happens if there is no younger brother, or if the younger brother is already married? In any case, the details are relatively unimportant and Jesus rebukes the Sadducees who try to pin him down with a complicated story based on this custom (read Matthew 22:23–33).

Genesis 39:1–23

From slavery to prison

For God's people, often the way up begins with a long downhill slope. Being in prison may be the prerequisite for being prime minister!

Joseph now begins to make a new life for himself in Egypt. Just as it appears that things are going well again, he receives yet another devastating blow; but the way he responds tells us much about his developing character.

Climbing the ladder (39:1–6a)

As 'captain of the guard', Potiphar holds a very responsible position among Pharaoh's officials, equivalent to that held by Nebuzaradan within Nebuchadnezzar's administration (2 Kings 25:8). In the providence of God, Potiphar buys Joseph from the Ishmaelites (verse 1); in this household Joseph will quickly become familiar with many of the Egyptian leaders. What is much more significant, though, is that 'the LORD was with him' (verses 2, 3), and, through Joseph, the Lord's blessing rests upon the household of Potiphar (verse 5).

It would be easy for Joseph to be in despair, but he quickly pulls himself out of any self-pity and gets on with the tasks assigned to him. He puts into practice the advice Paul later gives to the slaves in the Ephesian church: 'Serve wholeheartedly, as if you were serving the Lord, not men …' (Ephesians 6:7). In this way Joseph becomes a channel of God's blessing to others, helping in a small way to fulfil the promise made to Abraham: 'all peoples on earth will be blessed through you' (12:3).

Potiphar quickly recognizes the qualities of this particular slave, and gives him a position of stewardship over his entire household (verses 4–5). This is again good training for the future task that God would entrust to Joseph, but it is not the only training he will need – certain lessons, for certain of God's saints, can only be learned in prison.

Resisting temptation (39:6b–10)

With responsibility comes temptation. And for Joseph, as for so many Christian leaders, there is the temptation towards immorality. Joseph is a young, single, attractive male, who has inherited the good looks of his mother (verse 6; compare 29:17). He is far from any family ties, a slave in a foreign country, and his master's wife wants to seduce him. It will be so easy for Joseph to rationalize why it does not matter if he gives in: no-one, except God, will know.

The strength of character Joseph shows in this situation is almost unexpected given his family background: we have just read of how his older brother Judah handled sexual temptation (38:15–18). But the irritating adolescent whom we met in chapter 37 has begun to be transformed, for Joseph refuses his master's wife (verse 8), and then repeatedly refuses her. Wisely, he tries to avoid her company (verse 10; compare 1 Corinthians 6:18).

Falsely accused (39:11–20a)

The inevitable happens. One day Potiphar's wife finds Joseph alone in the house (verse 11), and when he rebuffs her advances and flees, her lust turns to hatred, and she makes an unjust accusation against him (verses 13–18). As in 37:23, 31, Joseph's garment is held in the hands of those who would do him harm, ready to be used deceptively as 'evidence'.

This whole story is echoed in that of Amnon and Tamar (2 Samuel 13), except that 'since he was stronger than she, he raped her' (verse 14). Otherwise there is the same lust, the same invitation 'Come to bed with me', the same refusal, and the same hatred afterwards. Tamar even has 'a richly ornamented robe' (verse 18) – the same Hebrew phrase that describes the robe of Joseph (Genesis 37:3) – and presumably hers is also now stained with blood.

Potiphar's anger may not be aimed against Joseph (verse 19); if he genuinely believes his wife, he would put Joseph to death. But the word of a slave can never overturn that of the master's wife, and Joseph is put in prison (verse 20a), although it may be that Potiphar, even there, keeps a fatherly eye upon him (compare 40:3).

The presence of the Lord (39:20b–23)

Later in Israel's history Moses will be brought up in Pharaoh's court, and then spend forty years in the desert before delivering his people (Exodus 2). David, too, will spend time at Saul's court (1 Samuel 18 – 20) before being in the wilderness for almost a decade (1 Samuel 21 – 26). And so Joseph, having been the master of Potiphar's household, now needs to be in a position of powerlessness, completely dependent upon God, before God can finally use him to save his people.

The temptation to despair must now be redoubled, but Joseph has an ability to climb above his circumstances. And he knows that even here the Lord is with him (verse 21), once again 'giving him success' in all things (verse 23; compare verse 3). Joseph is a born administrator. Having entered Potiphar's house as a slave, he was soon running it, and now, as a prisoner, he is soon organizing the whole prison (verse 22). This is again a part of his training, for soon he will be running the whole country!

Questions

1. How can we cultivate an attitude of rising above our circumstances when we are the victims of injustice?
2. How can your church encourage your young people to have the strength of character to resist temptation?
3. What can those who aspire to leadership learn from the story of Joseph?

Genesis 40:1–23
Forgotten!

Sometimes, when we think it can't get any worse, it does. But that may be the darkness before the dawn: one day the sun will rise again.

'Joseph, what can be worse than being sold into slavery by your own family? And then being thrown into prison in a foreign country on a false charge?'
'Being forgotten.'

Fellow prisoners (40:1–8)

The prison where Joseph is being held is in the house he has been in charge of (verses 3, 7). When two more prisoners arrive, 'the captain of the guard' – presumably still Potiphar (39:1) – gives them into Joseph's care (verse 4).

Both men held responsible positions. The cupbearer would taste any drink offered to the king as a precaution against poisoning, but would himself have the best opportunity for poisoning the king! (Nehemiah holds this position in the court of Artaxerxes, Nehemiah 1:11b; 2:1.) The baker would obviously be responsible for the king's daily bread. It is unlikely that either has committed a serious crime, but something as minor as spilling the wine or burning the toast. These will have been enough to send them into custody until the king happens to remember them again. Nehemiah is fearful of the king's anger simply for having a sad expression on his face (Nehemiah 2:1–3)!

Both men have a significant dream one night (verse 5), and Joseph, refusing to dwell on his own troubles, and concerned for their welfare, immediately notices the difference in their faces (verses 6–7). Interpreting dreams was a major business in ancient Egypt, and it would be common to go to a priest for an interpretation whenever appropriate. The two officials are sad because in their present situation they do not have this access (verse 8a), and must carry with them the burden of an uninterpreted dream. But Joseph has had two significant dreams himself: he knows what they have experienced and is confident that God will give him the interpretation (verse 8b).

The dreams (40:9–19)

The cupbearer sees in his dream a symbolic portrayal of himself back in his old job, pouring wine out for Pharaoh. Joseph indicates that this will indeed happen, within three days (verses 9–13).

Joseph sees that this might provide an opportunity for his release. He cannot appeal to Potiphar for mercy, as Potiphar cannot be seen to have released a man commonly believed to have molested his wife – thus Joseph's only hope is to appeal to Pharaoh. But to do this he has to have someone speak to Pharaoh on his behalf: as a foreigner he does not have anyone who can perform this function. But the cupbearer, a man who would speak to Pharaoh daily, now knows of the Hebrew prisoner's plight, and Joseph appeals to be remembered (verses 14–15).

The baker also sees himself back in his old job, taking baskets of bread to Pharaoh, but the birds are eating from the top basket (verses 16–17). Joseph prophesies that the baker will hang (verses 18–19).

The fulfilment (40:20–23)

Both dreams are fulfilled on the third day – note the gallows humour in verses 21–22, where the writer plays with the idea that each of their heads is 'lifted up'! The conclusion to the story is, however, emphatic. Phrased both positively and negatively (compare 11:30), we are left in no doubt that Joseph is a long way from the mind of the cupbearer (verse 23), and we learn from 41:1 that this goes on for two years. These must have been the toughest two years of all for Joseph. It is easier to reconcile oneself to life in prison if there is no hope of release, than if one constantly thinks that release might be around the corner. Most difficult of all to bear is the hope.

There may be situations in your own life in which you are seeking for God to act, for example for healing, or the conversion of a loved one, or a new move of God's Spirit in your church or community. There are sometimes moments when it appears that he is acting, but then nothing more happens, and you can begin to understand Joseph's feelings. It may be that these situations occur to draw us nearer to God, to find our comfort in him rather than in manifestations of his power.

Questions

1. Try to think of situations where you have promised to do something, but have 'forgotten'. What can you do to put the situation right?
2. If there is a prison in your area, what can your church do to support those who seek to bring a Christian witness into that place?
3. What can you do to help those imprisoned unjustly, in your own country or elsewhere, and especially those who have no-one else to speak up for them?

Genesis 41:1–57

From prison to Prime Minister

Those who honour God he will also honour, in his own time and in his own way.

 Joseph has had two dreams in his youth which are as yet unfulfilled (37:5–11). He has interpreted the two dreams of the cupbearer and the baker, both of which are fulfilled three days later (chapter 40). Now Pharaoh has two dreams, whose fulfilment will also lead to the fulfilment of the dreams from Joseph's youth.

Cows and corn (41:1–8)

It is hard for us to imagine exactly what the people of Egypt felt about Pharaoh. In their eyes, he was no ordinary man, but a representative of the gods, whose word was binding and whose dreams might affect the destiny of their entire country. Equally, the Nile was no ordinary river, and was worshipped as a god. Without the Nile, Egypt would die, and every year the behaviour of the river would be precisely noted to discover the attitude of the gods towards them. Cows too were no 'ordinary' animals. They were a national symbol of Egypt itself (and also of one of the Egyptian gods, Isis). Furthermore, grain was crucial to Egypt's economy.

Thus when Pharaoh recounts a dream about cows coming up from the Nile, seven sleek and seven ugly, and the ugly eat the sleek – a nightmarish image for Pharaoh which awakens him (verses 1–4) – all Egypt is anxious about the interpretation (verse 8). And the more so, when he recounts a second dream: seven thin ears of corn swallow up seven healthy ears (verses 5–7). None of the explanations of the experts rings true (verse 8).

Joseph remembered (41:9–32)

The cupbearer, reminded by the dreams, finally tells Pharaoh about Joseph (verses 9–13), the newly clean-shaven Joseph (verse 14) – for Egyptians, beards were anathema – enters Pharaoh's presence. Joseph is again confident of God's help in interpreting the dreams (verse 16), and Pharaoh recounts them once more (verses 17–24).

This is the moment for which God has been preparing Joseph for the previous thirteen years – perhaps for the whole of his life. Joseph's adolescent arrogance has now matured into confidence, and his natural wisdom and understanding have been refined by a deep knowledge of his dependence upon God. He is ready for the task to which he has been called, and eloquently explains the interpretation of the dreams to Pharaoh (verses 25–32): seven years of plenty will be followed by seven years of famine.

Joseph's promotion (41:33–45)

Not wanting to waste the opportunity, Joseph confidently continues by outlining a plan to store up food from the years of plenty in order to survive the years of famine (verses 33–36). It would be surprising for 'a fifth' of the harvest (verse 34 NIV) to be sufficient to cover the later need, but the Hebrew verb is ambiguous and may be better translated 'to *organize* the harvest of Egypt …', leaving the precise proportion to be decided later.

Pharaoh is impressed by Joseph's wisdom, and immediately places him in charge of the plan the young Hebrew has proposed (verses 37–43). Joseph is next given Egyptian clothing (verse 42), an Egyptian name (of unclear meaning) and marries a wife from the Egyptian aristocracy (verse 45). Such a promotion for a foreigner was not unprecedented in Egyptian history; indeed, this whole story might have occurred during the time of the Hyksos, who, like Joseph, were Semites. These invaders ruled Egypt from about 1650–1540 BC.

More than a thousand years later, another young Israelite taken by force from his homeland will stand before a pagan king and have to tell the king *what his dream has been*, as well as giving the interpretation! The man is Daniel (see Daniel 2), perhaps a wiser man than Joseph, but with the same awareness of his dependence upon God, and with the same calling of being placed by God within the government of a pagan, foreign country in order to help his people in their moment of need. Such men and women still exist – they deserve our respect and need our prayers.

Years of plenty (41:46–57)

Joseph, confident of the dream's interpretation, swings into action and stores up vast quantities of grain (verses 46–49). His own family is also fruitful, as his wife bears him two sons, Manasseh and Ephraim (verses 50–52), whom he hopes will help him to forget the problems of the past.

After seven years the easier part of Joseph's job is at an end; then, as the famine begins, he has to ensure a fair and adequate distribution of grain both to his own people and to refugees from other countries (verses 53–57). But as we have seen, God has been training him all along for this administrative task, and to those who serve him faithfully in small tasks, he will later entrust much greater tasks (Matthew 25:21).

Questions

1. How much should we 'store up grain' for the future and how much should we depend on God to give us what we need on a daily basis (compare Matthew 6:11)?
2. Given Joseph's example, how far do you think cross-cultural workers from your church should take on board the culture of the people among whom they are working?
3. In view of the examples of Joseph and Daniel, what advice would you give a Christian working in an ungodly government who seeks to be 'salt and light' there?

Genesis 42:1–38

Preparing the ground for reconciliation

Forgiveness and reconciliation involves working through the events of the past, rather than ignoring them.

It must have occurred to Joseph that his own family would need to come to Egypt for grain, and he must have wondered how he would deal with them. And then, at last, the day arrived.

Into Egypt (42:1–5)

Jacob's sons appear nervous about going to Egypt to get grain, perhaps because the family connections with Egypt have not been happy ones (compare 12:10–20; 26:2). They are unsure how their father will react (verse 1), but Jacob is much more proactive than they are. He tells them to get going (verse 2), but they are not to take Benjamin, who is pointedly referred to as 'Joseph's brother' (verse 4). The harm Jacob is concerned about (verse 4) is not named, but one wonders whether he fears that it might come from the brothers themselves.

'You are spies!' (42:6–17)

The focus now moves to Egypt, and we see the arrival of the brothers from Joseph's perspective. He immediately recognizes them (verses 7–8), and remembers his dreams (verse 9), but, unsurprisingly, they only perceive a stranger. It often happens that we fail at first to recognize someone when we meet them in a totally unexpected context, and in this case over twenty years have gone by: Joseph is clean-shaven, dressed in Egyptian clothing and speaking a foreign language!

The next few chapters give in considerable detail the 'game' Joseph plays with his brothers, but he is not simply trying to 'get his own back'. The process he takes them through is as difficult (but as necessary) for him as for his brothers; three times he breaks down and weeps (42:24; 43:30; 45:1–2). The experience clearly brings back painful memories of the traumatic events of his youth, which he has desperately tried to forget.

Joseph needs to work out his own relationship to his brothers. Real forgiveness does not ignore the past, nor pretend that it did not happen – it has to acknowledge the reality of what has occurred. He is also testing them, to find out if their betrayal of him twenty years before has permanently changed them. He wants to bring them into a situation where he can observe their reaction when Benjamin is threatened, and to see whether they are willing to acknowledge their guilt for their treatment of him. To do this he will frequently place them in situations that parallel the earlier events.

Joseph's initial reaction may have been harsh (verse 7), because neither his father nor Benjamin is with the brothers. For all Joseph knows, despite his dreams (37:5–11), his father may be dead and Benjamin also sold. He thus accuses them of spying, which in his adolescence Joseph has himself been guilty of (37:2). Their defence reveals that Benjamin is safe and his father alive (verse 13), but, to be sure, Joseph wants to see Benjamin for himself (verse 15). Perhaps in order to give them time to work things through, he then puts them in prison, again paralleling his own experience, and waits a few days (verse 17).

Revelations from the past (42:18–26)

Joseph's initial plan to send just one brother back (verse 16) is revised to spare his father more pain. Instead, just one brother is kept as a hostage (verse 19). This provokes a discussion among the brothers in which Joseph learns some interesting facts (the brothers, of course, do not realize that he understands Hebrew; see verse 23).

First, he learns that his brothers still feel guilt for what they have done, and they see what is happening to them as a punishment (verse 21). Second, Reuben had no part in the plot (verse 22) – indeed, perhaps the brothers never told Reuben what had actually happened (compare 37:29–30). Given Reuben's innocence, Joseph takes Simeon, the second eldest, as the hostage (verse 24). Joseph then secretly places their silver back into their bags. They sold him for silver (37:28) and he wants to test how much they value it. Will they keep the silver and leave Simeon to his fate, or return it honestly (verses 25–26)?

The return to Canaan (42:27–38)

The discovery of the returned silver leaves the brothers even more disorientated than before (verses 27–28). Bewildered and fearful, they return to their father (verse 29) and tell him an abbreviated version of all that has happened – missing out the details that they have been imprisoned for three days, that they feared that this was a punishment for their treatment of Joseph, and that Simeon has been bound (verses 30–34).

But once before they had returned without a brother, and with pockets full of silver; now it is happening again. Jacob is unsure whether to believe their explanation: he might well think that they have sold Simeon (verse 36). Reuben, struggling to get back on good terms with his father (compare 35:22; 37:21–22), overreacts, and is ignored. But the situation remains as a stalemate, with Jacob again insensitively referring to Benjamin as his 'only' son (verse 38). But time, and hunger, will change matters.

Questions

---

1. If we have been sinned against, what steps need to be gone through before we can truly have a restored relationship?
2. How can the church support those who have suffered as a result of dysfunctional family relationships, and help them to forgive those who have hurt them?
3. Who do you think has the responsibility to ask for forgiveness for 'national sins' in the past, and how far back should the process go?

Sometimes in life we have to continue to act, in faith, even when we don't know the whole story or what our part is in it.

The ongoing famine gradually wears away Jacob's resolution. It forces him to make ever more painful decisions, although ultimately, unknown to him, it will lead to the greatest reunion of his life (46:29).

Jacob's defences crumble (43:1–14)

Jacob still hopes against hope that he can avoid sending Benjamin to Egypt: can his sons, he suggests, just go and buy 'a little more food' (verse 2)?

This is a delicate situation. The brothers know that they *have* to take Benjamin with them, and they know that this will hurt their father enormously. They need to persuade him to give his permission, and now the one who takes charge is Judah. Reuben's desperate overreaction (42:37) simply echoes Lot's willingness to put his own children in danger (19:8), demonstrating his lack of wisdom. The leadership of the brothers has been moving towards Judah ever since they followed his plan to sell Joseph (37:27), but now, after the bereavement and humiliation of chapter 38, instead of leading them into a sin, his leadership gifts can be used more wisely.

Judah calmly and patiently explains the situation to his father (verses 3–5) and states that he will take personal responsibility for the lad, while at the same time emphasizing the urgency of the situation (verses 8–10). Note how he uses Jacob's own phrase 'that we may live and not die' (42:2) in his reply (verse 8). There are times when we may have to persuade someone to make a decision that we know is in their best interest, but which they are unwilling to make. Judah's wise realism, compassion and willingness to take the responsibility for the decision provide us with a good model.

In the end, as he has no choice, Jacob reluctantly agrees, and, like his earlier gifts to Esau (32:13–21), instructs that such gifts as are possible in a famine situation should be taken to the Egyptian overseer to appease his anger (verses 11–12). The gifts he chooses (verse 11) duplicate the items carried by the Ishmaelite traders (37:25), unconsciously adding to the brothers' sense of *déjà vu*. Jacob finally commits them to God, resigned, if necessary, to further bereavement (verse 14).

Jacob is following in the footsteps of the earlier patriarchs: each comes to a point where he needs to commit his child to God – a test of faith that cuts to the heart. Abraham had to send Ishmael into danger (21:8–14), and to be willing to sacrifice Isaac (chapter 22); Isaac had to allow Jacob to flee (28:1–5), not knowing if he would see him again (compare 27:2, 41); and Jacob in turn now has to let Benjamin go. It is encouraging that, having taken their hands off their children, these parents are eventually reunited with their child – God has, indeed, had his hand upon them.

Meeting Joseph's steward (43:15–25)

Joseph, having made sure that Benjamin is with them, instructs his steward to take them to his house for a meal (verses 15–16). The brothers assume that they are about to be arrested and enslaved for failing to pay for their first load of grain (verses 17–18). They need to prove their innocence quickly. Surrounding the steward, they explain what had happened – perhaps through an interpreter, although the steward may well understand at least some Hebrew (verses 19–22). The steward puts their minds at rest, tells them that they are simply Joseph's guests (verse 25), and brings Simeon out to them (verse 23). They prepare themselves for lunch and get their gifts ready for Joseph (verses 24–25). In addition Joseph is still trying to keep his brothers on edge by doing the unexpected. His unexpected hospitality probably confuses them as much as their unexpected prison sentence on their first visit (42:17). What we are really like is often best revealed when we are not in control of a situation, and we have to act within an apparently bizarre context.

Fear often causes us to feel that situations are worse than they really are, and the Bible often repeats the command 'Do not be afraid'. Fear distorts our perception of a situation and indicates a lack of trust in God, but we must also remember that God speaks such words, sometimes gently and sometimes sternly, to those who *are* afraid, because his ongoing desire is for a relationship with us in which fear has no place.

Honouring Benjamin (43:26–34)

When Joseph asks about his father (verse 27) his brothers assume he is only being courteous – but actually he is desperately concerned for he must know that the shock of having to say farewell to Rachel's other son will have been hard for Jacob to bear. For Joseph, meeting his closest brother again is itself an overwhelming experience, and again he weeps (verses 29–30).

Although Joseph has tried to become 'Egyptianized', he has never been allowed to forget his ethnic origin, for he has always been served his food alone (verse 32). This must have been difficult, for if it were not for Joseph the Egyptians would have had no food to eat at all! But all cross-cultural workers must feel the same emotions at times; there will always be moments when they are reminded that they are foreigners, even when they have brought God's love to a people.

Joseph continues to be an enigma to his brothers, honouring Benjamin (verse 34) and seating them in the order of their ages (verse 33), thus giving them the illusion that they can keep no secrets from him (compare 44:15). It is, after all, when you are convinced that the other person knows the whole truth anyway that you can be most honest with them. They drink freely with him (verse 34), imagining that the worst is over, but making it more plausible that they have had the opportunity to steal his cup (44:5).

Questions

1. What people in your life do you need to take your hands off, committing them in faith to the Lord?
2. In what innovative ways might your church encourage cross-cultural workers that you know about, enabling them to bear the pain of being 'a stranger in a strange land' more easily?
3. How might you change national customs which have the effect of alienating those of other cultural backgrounds?

Genesis 44:1–34

True repentance

One measure of greatness is a desire to atone for sins committed in the past.

The brothers must have left Joseph's house astonished by their change of fortune. Instead of being arrested, they have enjoyed the hospitality of the Egyptian governor, they have been allowed to keep the silver discovered in their sacks, Simeon has been restored to them, and they are returning to Jacob with Benjamin safe and sound.

But the real test is still to come. Joseph deliberately favours Benjamin (43:34) to bring to the surface any jealousy the brothers might still be harbouring, before arresting Benjamin for theft. This will be the crucial moment: will the brothers treat Benjamin as they treated Joseph all those years before, when he was the 'favourite', or will they be willing to sacrifice themselves on Benjamin's behalf?

Plotting behind the scenes (44:1–5)

Again the brothers' silver is returned (verse 1; compare 42:25). In the dreamlike logic of these episodes it is as if they will be unable to get rid of their silver until they have also got rid of their guilt, for they received silver when they incurred that guilt (37:28). In addition, Joseph's own silver cup is placed in Benjamin's sack (verse 2). This kind of cup also had religious significance, as liquids would often be used in divination ceremonies. Thus in verse 5 Joseph keeps up the pretence of being a typical Egyptian overlord, but we are not expected to believe that he himself engaged in such divination.

The steward then leaves with his instructions (verses 4–5), setting the brothers up for their final confrontation with him.

The accusation (44:6–13)

The brothers, naturally, defend their innocence. They were hardly likely to have jeopardized their good fortune with such an action, were they? They had even attempted to return the silver they found the first time, as a demonstration of their innocence (verses 6–8).

When Jacob was pursued by Laban and accused of stealing the household gods, he was so confident of his innocence that he said that, when found, the culprit would die (31:32) – little knowing the danger in which he was placing Rachel. Jacob's sons now repeat Jacob's words (verse 9); little knowing the danger in which they are placing Rachel's son. The steward tones down their suggestion; only the guilty man will be taken. And he will not die, but become a slave (verse 10), reminiscent of the brothers' decision not to kill Joseph but to sell him into slavery (37:26–27).

Of course, no two stories are identical; Rachel was guilty of theft, but got away with it (31:35); Benjamin is innocent, but the cup is finally found in his sack (verse 12). It is not clear whether the brothers regard Benjamin as guilty (thus giving them another reason to leave him in the lurch), or whether this is seen merely as another bizarre twist of fate. Either way, they mourn yet another change in their fortune, tearing their clothes (verse 13; compare 37:34), and return to the city (verse 13).

Judah's defence (44:14–34)

Judah had persuaded Jacob to allow Benjamin to come (43:3–5, 8–10), and having assumed this responsibility, he courageously does not shy away from bearing the consequences in the face of catastrophe. In the present situation Judah knows that the circumstantial evidence is overwhelming and the best he can hope for is that they will all be slaves with Benjamin (verse 16). At least he will not have to look his father in the eye again. But Joseph protests that his justice will not allow him to accept this offer, and he twists the knife one final time. Only Benjamin will stay; the rest can leave (verse 17).

Judah's response – the longest speech in Genesis – is magnificent. The whole speech is completely focused on their father, who is mentioned fourteen times. Judah has seen his father hurt once (37:34), and cannot bear to do so again: Jacob will surely die if Benjamin does not return (verse 31). Judah finally accepts that his father's favouritism (verses 20, 27), which has so hurt him and come so near to destroying the family, is a part of the father he must love and sacrifice himself for. Indeed, Jacob's love for Benjamin is the reason why Judah must make this sacrifice.

Judah had suggested selling Joseph into slavery (37:26), and Judah concludes his speech (unknowingly addressed to Joseph!) by offering to go into slavery himself in order to save Joseph's brother (verse 33). The appeal is irresistible, although somewhat ironical. The Egyptians would see an innocent man offering to take the punishment for one who was guilty; Joseph would see a guilty man offering to take the punishment for someone who was innocent!

Leadership among God's people does not mean that one never sins, but that one genuinely repents of sins committed. And true repentance for sin demonstrates a willingness to do everything possible to prevent the situation happening again, and to shoulder the responsibility and the blame. This is why, even though his sins are at least as great as his brothers', ultimately Judah will receive 'the ruler's staff' (49:10). Like his descendant David, he is capable of great sins; but is also capable of great and genuine remorse (compare Psalm 51). Judah learnt a lesson from his daughter-in-law Tamar (38:26) that he never forgot.

Questions

1. In what sorts of situations might you be willing to bear the punishment for another person?
2. What space is given in your church for public repentance, or is repentance purely a personal matter between an individual and God?
3. List Judah's leadership qualities. Which of these, if any, do you see in the leaders of your nation?

Sometimes plans for reconciliation do work out well, and it is right to rejoice and to plan for the future on the basis of this restored relationship.

Judah cannot know how deeply his speech (44:18–34), and perhaps especially the references to his father, are affecting the man who stands before him. He hopes, perhaps, that the image of a grieving patriarchal figure will soften the Egyptian's stance from one of justice to one of compassion, little knowing that every detail of the portrait is already etched on Joseph's heart (compare verse 3).

The revelation (45: 1–15)

Joseph can keep up the pretence no longer (verse 1a). Indeed, there is no need, as the foundations for reconciliation are now securely laid. Joseph dismisses his attendants (verse 1b) and for the first time since that day at Dothan (37:17–28), he is alone with his brothers. He weeps (verse 2), and reveals his identity (verse 3), giving his brothers a massive shock! They are dumbfounded and terrified (verse 3), as if they have seen a ghost (compare Mark 6:49–50).

In a different context Jesus encourages Thomas to touch him in order to put his doubts at rest (John 20:27). Similarly Joseph encourages his brothers to gather round him, and he reaffirms his identity (verse 4a), for a closing of the physical distance between them naturally helps to bridge the psychological distance. It is impossible to ignore the fact that they have sold him into Egypt (verse 4b), but Joseph has worked through his anger and distress, and has learned to see the part this event has played in God's bigger plan. Three times he tells them it was God who sent him into Egypt (verses 5, 7, 8), to accomplish his purpose of saving life. In the light of their obvious repentance, Joseph has completely forgiven them, and wants them to be able to forgive themselves as well so that their relationship can now begin afresh (verse 5).

Joseph (always the administrator) then explains to his brothers that there are still five years of famine left (verse 6) and it is wise for them to come and join him in Egypt (verses 9–11). Their reconciliation is publicly complete, although the brothers take a long time to believe that Joseph has forgiven them (compare 50:15). They weep together, and then catch up with two decades' worth of news about one another (verses 14–15).

The offer (45:16–24)

Pharaoh's household have already heard rumours that Joseph is weeping in the presence of his visitors (verse 2). When they hear that Joseph's family have come, they are genuinely glad. Pharaoh immediately promises that they will be well provided for (verses 17–18), and appropriate transport is made available (verses 19–20). Joseph equips the group adequately and Benjamin, lavishly, perhaps in compensation for the treatment the youngest brother has received (verse 22). The reversal is complete, for Joseph, who has twice been stripped of his garments, and has received clothing from Pharaoh (41:42), is now in a position to give garments to others (verse 22). And as his father had sent gifts to him (43:11), so he now sends gifts to his father (verse 23).

The unbelievable news! (45:25–28)

The brothers must wonder how they will break the news to their father. Will they tell him about their betrayal of Joseph twenty-two years before? Does he need to know what happened? Will Joseph ever tell his father the whole story, or can they rely on him to keep silent? In the end, they simply blurt out two pieces of impossible news together, 'Joseph is alive! Actually he is the ruler of Egypt!' Jacob is stunned (verse 26), but as they expand on their story he is finally persuaded that they are speaking the truth, and he makes the momentous decision to go to Egypt (verses 27–28).

It is difficult for Christians to read this story without seeing in it a dim foreshadowing of the reconciliation Christ brought to the earth. Of course the details are different, but like Judah, we need to repent and to receive the forgiveness of one whom we have sinned against, one whom we might meet in unexpected places, times and circumstances. We, too, are called to begin a new life on the basis of our restored relationship. But we must go a step further: we have to forgive others in the same way that we ourselves have received forgiveness (Matthew 18:23–35).

Questions

1. In what ways can you trace the hand of God in situations which, at the time, were highly traumatic?
2. The Lord's supper ought to be a place for celebrating reconciliation between Christians, as well as between us and the Lord. How might your church enable this to occur more easily?
3. How can Christians support efforts to reduce the impact of famine in our world, and what should our motivation be?

Genesis 46:1 – 47:12
A new beginning

When we are faced with a major change, it is good to 'take stock' of where we are, where we have come from and where we are going.

This is a key moment in Israel's history: the chosen family are about to leave the land God promised to Abraham's descendants (12:7); and it is time to take stock and prepare for this new start.

Revisiting Beersheba (46:1–7)

The 25-mile route from Hebron to Beersheba was familiar to all of the patriarchs; Jacob himself had fled from Beersheba many years before (28:10). All sorts of memories would be stirred up and, as Jacob passes through the town, he offers sacrifices to 'the God of his father Isaac'. Isaac, who died just ten years before (35:28), was forbidden to enter Egypt during a similar famine (26:2) and ended up in Beersheba, where he had a vision of God (26:23–24). Jacob's sacrifice, perhaps offered on the altar built by his father (26:25), is a thanksgiving to God for his protection over the previous half-century, a recommitment of his future to God as he enters yet another new phase in his life, and also an honouring of his father.

Like his father, he receives a vision of God (verse 2). God affirms that his presence with the family will continue, even in Egypt, and that Joseph will be present when Jacob dies (verse 4). With renewed confidence the trip to Egypt continues (verses 5–7), but despite Pharaoh's suggestion (45:20), they take their familiar possessions with them (verse 6): it is always good to retain some continuity in times of change.

The roll-call (46:8–27)

The narrator then provides a list of the family members. The number seventy implies the completeness or totality of the family that makes the journey to Egypt. There are seventy names in the 'Table of Nations' (chapter 10), seventy male descendants in the first four generations of Terah's family (chapters 11 – 35), seventy names linked with Esau (chapter 36), and now seventy names are listed in Jacob's family tree (verse 27). To achieve this total the wives, and virtually all the 'daughters and granddaughters' mentioned in verse 7 are excluded, so that the list ultimately contains sixty-eight males and two females, Dinah (verse 15) and Serah (verse 17).

During Jacob's lifetime the people of Israel have increased from one, to twelve, to seventy, the stages corresponding to when he fled from Canaan (28:10), when he returned (chapter 32), and now as he leaves again for Egypt. Interestingly, these same figures reoccur in the Gospels: Jesus, one person, chooses twelve 'apostles' (Luke 6:13), and later sends out a group of seventy 'disciples' (Luke 10:1, 17, NIV footnote).

Settling in Goshen (46:28 – 47:12)

When they arrive in Goshen, Joseph goes to meet them, and the second great reunion of Jacob's life occurs. He spent twenty years in Haran before his reconciliation with Esau (chapter 33), and twenty-two years imagining that Joseph was dead, before now being reunited. Not surprisingly, the tears, at least on Joseph's part, fall for a long time (verse 29).

Joseph then resumes the role of diplomat. Earlier he suggested to his brothers that the family would be given land in Goshen (45:10), which lay to the east of the main Egyptian population centres, an excellent area for pasturage. Joseph's offer needs to be ratified by Pharaoh, however, and he also needs to show Pharaoh that he has no intention of incorporating his family into the Egyptian civil service. His brothers will continue their previous occupation of tending livestock, and especially sheep, and will therefore not be a threat to established interests. All they require is land for pasturage. Joseph warns his brothers that the Egyptians are prejudiced against shepherds, but this can work in their favour: by admitting their occupation, they will be more likely to get the appropriate land (verse 34).

Joseph presents five brothers (more would be undignified) to Pharaoh, and they tell him that they are shepherds; 'just as our fathers were' (verse 3) implies that they have no ambition to reach higher. Uncomfortable with the silence that follows, they then mention that they are only intending to stay for the duration of the famine, and explicitly state that they would like to stay in Goshen (verse 4). Pharaoh regally bestows his favour on them through Joseph; he gladly gives them land in Goshen and, aware that they are no threat, allows some of them to have an official position (verses 5–6).

After this somewhat tense scene, Jacob is brought before Pharaoh (verse 7). Now a dignified, patriarchal figure, he blesses Pharaoh (compare Jeremiah 29:7). There was great respect for the elderly in Egypt, and Pharaoh desires to identify with this man, asking him his age (verse 8). Jacob, though, does not want to glory in this and, after blessing Pharaoh once more, leaves (verses 9–10).

Questions

1. In what ways might we give appropriate honour to our parents, even after they die?
2. How can we balance the need for continuity with the need to make fresh beginnings in our churches?
3. How can the church encourage our own society to give appropriate help to the refugees within our nation?

Genesis 47:13 – 48:22

Recalling the past, blessing the future

Despite our distracting surroundings, we should never forget where our true home is and where our 'citizenship' ultimately lies.

Jacob's family comes to Egypt after two years of the famine, but faced a further five years (45:6, 11). Joseph, however, ensures that they have adequate provisions (47:12).

Who owns the land? (47:13–27)

Joseph functions as Pharaoh's deputy and performs his job efficiently. Although the people are gradually reduced to poverty, they are grateful that at least their lives are saved (verse 25). When their money is used up (verse 14), they exchange their capital assets – their livestock (verses 16–17), and then their land – for grain (verses 18–21). The net result is that Pharaoh owns the entire land, with his subjects merely tenants. When Joseph gives the people a final handout of seed to begin planting again after the famine has ended, he establishes a law that 20 per cent of the produce should be given to Pharaoh, thus ensuring the future prosperity of the dynasty (verses 23–24).

The two exceptions to this poverty are the priestly classes (verses 22, 26b), whose special arrangement with Pharaoh gives them some independence, and the Israelites, who have settled in Goshen and even 'acquired property there' (verse 27). This shows God's blessing upon them, but also hints that it may not be so easy for them to leave at the end of the famine as they have intimated (47:4).

The details of the ownership of land and property in Egypt provide a model for the Israelites when they eventually return to the land God promised to give them. The land is God's land, not theirs; they are merely his tenants and servants (Leviticus 25:23, 55). Thus God has the right to demand that they use the land and its produce in a way that reflects his character: with justice and generosity towards the poor (for example Deuteronomy 15:11). If they do not do so, the land will 'vomit' them out (Leviticus 18:28).

Jacob's request (47:28–31)

The seventeen years that Jacob lives in Egypt with Joseph (verse 28) match the seventeen years they had spent together in Canaan (37:2). Jacob knows it is time to die, and asks Joseph to swear solemnly (verse 29; compare 24:2) to bury him with Abraham and Isaac in the cave of Machpelah, near Hebron (25:9; 35:29). Of course Joseph agrees (verse 31). It is symbolically important that the patriarchs are buried in the land God promised them. Even in death, they are acting as models for the generations to come, motivating them to return to the land when absent from it.

Jacob blesses Ephraim and Manasseh (48:1–22)

Farewell speeches are important. They are full of significant statements, which a lifetime's wisdom has helped to shape. Deuteronomy, for example, is Moses' farewell speech to the nation, while John records Jesus' farewell speech at length (John 13 – 17). Here we have the farewell speeches of Jacob.

Jacob grew up as a younger son who contrived to trick his blind father into blessing him rather than Esau (chapter 27). Now it is his turn to bless Ephraim and Manasseh, and once again it will be the younger brother who receives the blessing (verse 19). But this time there will be no trickery. Jacob begins by recalling God's promise to him in the land of Canaan (verses 3–4). He then legally 'adopts' Ephraim and Manasseh (verse 5); later in Israel's history each of these will be counted as a separate tribe and be given their own land. (There were still only twelve tribal territories, however, as the tribe of Levi was not given land but was set aside for duties in the tabernacle.)

As Jacob ponders the future of Joseph's sons – Rachel's grandsons – his mind wanders back to the death of Rachel, the great sorrow of his life (verse 7). When he returns to the present, his poor sight (verse 10) prevents him from recognizing Ephraim and Manasseh (verse 8) – unless these verses (8–9) are part of a legal adoption ceremony. Either way, his desire is to bless them, and as he holds them he again reminisces about the past and about the unexpected joy God has given him in his old age (verse 11).

Joseph directs Manasseh, the firstborn, towards Jacob's right hand, but Jacob crosses his arms and, placing his right hand on Ephraim (verses 12–14), begins a blessing that recalls God's faithfulness to him and connects the past with the future. He calls upon Abraham's God to fulfil in these young men the promises made to Abraham (verses 15–16).

There are things Jacob has been working through for the whole of his life, and which he understands much better than Joseph ever will; thus, despite Joseph's protest (verses 17–18), the wise old man knows in the very fibre of his being that it is the younger son who will be the greater (verses 19–20). Following the pattern thus far in Genesis, how can it be otherwise?

Jacob finally gives Joseph a special plot of land, fought for in an otherwise unrecorded incident (verse 22), reminding his son that God will indeed take him back to Canaan (verse 21).

Questions

1. If you knew that the day of your death was not far away, what sort of things would you want to include in a farewell speech to those you love?
2. How can we show the elderly within our churches the same care, respect and patience that Joseph and his sons show their father?
3. How can we take our responsibility as stewards of the earth's resources more seriously?

Genesis 49:1–28

Glimpses of the future

How *we* act is often significant in shaping how our children and our children's children will also act.

The special 'audience' given to Joseph's sons is highly significant. We have explored the ongoing tension between the brothers as to who will get the firstborn rights. Will it be Reuben? – but he slept with Bilhah (35:22).

Will it be Simeon or Levi? – but they attacked the Shechemites (chapter 34). Will it be Judah, or Joseph? In fact Jacob solves the problem in his own way: by adopting Ephraim and Manasseh, making them like 'Reuben and Simeon' (48:5), and by blessing them first, he in effect gives the firstborn rights to them (read 1 Chronicles 5:1–2)!

Nevertheless the rest of Jacob's sons also receive from their father their own 'farewell message', focusing on and directing the future of their tribes (verses 1–2, 28). These are recorded for us here. Many of the sayings involve elaborate Hebrew puns based on their names, and other plays upon words, but you will need to refer to a larger commentary for explanations of these and other difficulties in the text and its interpretation.

The sons of Leah (49:3–15)

Reuben is the firstborn. Jacob's initial description of him (verse 3) builds up a noble portrait that is highly ironical, and makes his downfall more pitiable (verse 4; compare 35:22). His instability and lack of patience tempted him to grasp for what was already his by right, but, like Adam, he loses everything. The tribe of Reuben inherited the land east of the Dead Sea, but were almost completely insignificant in the later history of Israel.

Simeon and *Levi* have a reputation for unnecessary violence (verses 5–7). Their actions in chapter 34 are typical and, in retrospect, it is not surprising that the other brothers withdraw from supporting their act of vengeance – their own father more or less disowns them (verse 6a). They will each be dispersed in Israel (verse 7b). The men of the tribe of Simeon rapidly declined during the years in the wilderness from 59,300 (Numbers 1:22–23) to 22,200 (Numbers 26:14), and were not mentioned when Moses blessed the tribes (Deuteronomy 33). Although allocated their own land in the south of Canaan, in practice the tribe quickly became absorbed into Judah (compare Joshua 19:1). The tribe of Levi was also 'scattered', but because of their (violent) support for Moses (a Levite; Exodus 2:1) at a critical moment (Exodus 32:26) they were 'set apart to the Lord' (Exodus 32:29). Instead of receiving an allotment of land they were given forty-eight cities scattered throughout Israel (Joshua 21), and their task was to look after the tabernacle (Numbers 1:47–53).

Judah receives his father's commission to rule over his brothers (verse 8). He has already demonstrated his ability as a leader, and this trend will continue in his descendants. King

David came from this tribe, as did Jesus (Matthew 1), the one 'to whom it [the sceptre] belongs' (verse 10; compare Numbers 24:17). The image of the lion (verse 9) was later applied by John to Jesus (Revelation 5:5). The vineyard imagery used in verses 11–12 was often used to describe Israel itself (for example Isaiah 5:1–7), especially in a time of peace (for example 1 Kings 4:25). Jesus also used the image in referring to Israel (for example Mark 12:1–12), although, significantly, he also applied it to himself: 'I am the true vine' (John 15:1).

We know virtually nothing of the personal history of *Zebulun* and *Issachar* (verses 13–15). These tribes later had adjacent territories in the north of Israel: Zebulun to the west, and Issachar to the south-west, of the Sea of Galilee. It is not clear exactly how these sayings relate to what we know of the future of these tribes.

The sons of the concubines (49:16–21)

The tribe of *Dan* (verses 16–19) left its allotted area between Judah and Ephraim and moved north of the Sea of Galilee, violently destroying an innocent town and introducing idolatry into Israel (Judges 17 – 18). It later became a centre of idol worship (1 Kings 12:29) and was excluded from the people of God in the lists given in 1 Chronicles 2 – 8 and Revelation 7:5–8. Thus there may be a sinister element to the description given by Jacob (verse 17), as he portrays the tribe as a serpent (compare 3:1).

The tribe of *Gad* (verse 19) settled east of the Jordan in Gilead, and was highly vulnerable to attack; but it developed a strong military tradition in response to this (for example 1 Chronicles 12:8–15).

The tribe of *Asher* (verse 20) settled in a rich, fertile area on the north-west coast of Israel.

Naphtali's territory was to the north of Zebulun, where it was also vulnerable to attack (for example 2 Kings 15:29). It is uncertain what the saying (verse 21) symbolizes.

The sons of Rachel (49:22–28)

Joseph receives the longest speech; notice again the recurrence of the 'vine' imagery (verse 22; compare verse 11), although the Hebrew for 'fruitful vine' may also be translated 'wild ass'. Verses 23–24 portray the difficulties he has faced during his life, which, with God's help, he has successfully overcome. As a result Joseph receives blessings from God (verse 25) and from his father (verse 26) which cover two important areas of life, agriculture and childbearing (verse 25b), each of which God cursed in 3:16–19. Finally Joseph is honoured as a 'prince' among his brothers (verse 26).

The animal imagery continues with *Benjamin*, who is described as a 'ravenous wolf'. Later this tribe was renowned for its military exploits (for example Judges 3:15; 1 Chronicles 12:2) as well as for producing Israel's first king (1 Samuel 9:1–2).

Questions

1. If you were to picture yourself as an animal, what would it be and why?
2. What sort of blessing, or legacy, would you like your church to leave to the next generation?
3. What influence does the past have on different national characteristics, and how might these be converted towards Christ?

Genesis 49:29 – 50:26

The end of the beginning

For each of us, the end of our human journey lies in a coffin. It is important that our final actions and words glorify God and leave behind peace and not strife.

The death of Jacob (49:29 – 50:3)

Jacob earlier instructed Joseph to bury him with his fathers in Canaan (47:29–31), and those instructions are now amplified in the presence of all of the brothers (verses 29–32). Jacob is lucid right to the end, giving precise details about the family burial site, and then naming those who already lie there, whom he is about to meet.

183

We learn for the first time that Leah has died while Jacob was in Canaan (verse 31b); in her death Jacob gives her the honour that perhaps he had never given her during her life. We know nothing of the relationship between Jacob and Leah after Rachel's death, but perhaps Jacob begins to recognize her qualities more than when she was playing second fiddle to Rachel in his affections. Whereas Rachel was buried near where she died, on the road to Bethlehem, about 15 miles from Mamre (35:19), Leah is given the honour of burial within the family tomb, on a par with Sarah and Rebekah, the other patriarchal wives; and it is alongside her that Jacob will be buried.

Jacob's final words (verse 32) sound strange, but they remind the brothers that the cave is legitimately theirs. Although a tiny part of the land, this cave is a tangible symbol of God's promise to give the whole of the land to Abraham's descendants.

In control until the end, Jacob draws his feet 'up into the bed' (verse 33) and dies. Joseph, who has indeed been present at Jacob's death (46:4), weeps (verse 1), before organizing the seventy-day mourning rituals. Jacob is highly honoured by the Egyptians, for even Pharaohs were publicly mourned for only seventy-two days. Embalming the body is not only an honour, but a practical necessity as the body will not be buried until considerably later, and in another country.

Jacob's burial (50:4–14)

Perhaps for some ceremonial reason connected with mourning, Joseph cannot directly enter Pharaoh's presence; he therefore requests indirectly through the court (verse 4) permission to bury his father in Canaan (verse 5). Of course permission is granted (verse 6) and many of Pharaoh's officials come too. The chariots and horsemen (verse 9) are a natural bodyguard for the Egyptian dignitaries (verse 7), for there is no fear that the Israelites will not return (unlike later in Exodus). While the Egyptians stay by the borders of Canaan (verse 11), Jacob's sons take the body of their father and lay it in the cave of Machpelah (verses 12–13). They then return to Egypt (verse 14).

Old wounds resurface (50:15–21)

Thirty-nine years have passed since his brothers sold Joseph into slavery, but the event has so scarred their lives that they still feel he might take revenge upon them after their father's death

(verse 15; compare Esau in 27:41). They therefore create a ficti-
tious message from their father to Joseph (verses 16–17). Joseph
knows exactly what they have done and weeps (verse 17b). He
weeps for the pain that his brothers have unnecessarily been
carrying within them for so many years, doubting his words of
forgiveness seventeen years earlier. He is grieved that they are
afraid of him and feel it necessary to approach him in such a
roundabout way; distressed because they feel he will use the
death of his father as the springboard for revenge; remorseful that
he had not seen their anxiety and dealt with it many years before.
Perhaps he also weeps again because his father and mother are
dead. There are times when it is right, and indeed holy, to weep.

His brothers then offer to be his slaves (verse 18), but Joseph
repeats to them his words of almost two decades before
(45:4–11), this time in a softer key: they need have no fear, and
their children, too, need not fear (verses 19–21).

Joseph's death (50:22–26)

Fifty-four years pass with no comment, except that Joseph sees
his children grow up, and then his grandchildren, and then his
great-grandchildren (verses 22–23). Joseph, too, reaches a vener-
able age, and appropriately dies at the ideal Egyptian age of 110.

Some, at least, of his brothers are still alive and, in a final
gesture of reconciliation and a final act of faith, Joseph commits
to them the burden of ensuring that his body will be taken back
to Canaan when God leads his people back (verses 24–25; compare Hebrews 11:22). After his death, Joseph too is embalmed,
and placed in 'a coffin in Egypt' (verse 26). Thus in Genesis we
have moved from creation to a coffin, and although God's
purposes for his people will continue through many centuries,
we have reached the end of the beginning.

Questions

1. How can we forgive ourselves for sins we know that the
   Lord, and others, have already forgiven us for?
2. In what little ways has God worked in your church,
   foreshadowing bigger things that he might do in the future?
3. Do the public burial and mourning rites within your society
   enable an appropriate level of grief to be expressed, and if not
   how might they be changed?

For further reading

Plenty of material is available if you want to read more widely about the book of Genesis.

A useful small-scale commentary is the Tyndale Old Testament Commentary by Derek Kidner (IVP, 1967). At a larger scale Gordon Wenham's two Word commentaries (Genesis 1 – 15; Genesis 16 – 50; Word Books, 1987, 1994) are excellent, as is J. Gerald Janzen's more theological commentary, *Abraham and all the Families of the Earth: A Commentary on the Book of Genesis 12 – 50* (Handsel Press, 1993). Robert Alter has written his own translation and introduction to the book from a more literary perspective, *Genesis* (Norton & Company, 1996). The two volumes on Genesis in The Bible Speaks Today series are also worth consulting: David Atkinson, *The Message of Genesis 1 – 11* (IVP, 1990); and Joyce Baldwin, *The Message of Genesis 12 – 50* (IVP, 1986).

The relationship between Genesis and science is discussed in numerous books, from different perspectives. The 'creationist' position is outlined in Henry Morris (ed.), *Scientific Creationism* (Creation-Life Publishers, 1974), and from this side of the Atlantic, E. H. Andrews, *God, Science and Evolution* (Evangelical Press, 1980). A more mainstream approach is represented by books such as Roger Forster and Paul Marston, *Reason, Science and Faith* (Monarch Books, 1999); Ernest Lucas, *Can we believe Genesis today?* (IVP, 2001; originally published as *Genesis Today* [Scripture Union, 1989]; and, on Genesis 1 – 3, Henri Blocher, *In the Beginning* (IVP, 1984). At a more philosophical level try John Polkinghorne, *Science and Creation* (SPCK, 1988).

Derek Burke (ed.), *Creation and Evolution* (IVP, 1985), is a collection of essays both for and against evolution; note also R. J. Berry, *God and Evolution* (Hodder & Stoughton, 1988).

The classic book in defence of a global flood is John Whitcomb and Henry Morris, *The Genesis Flood* (Presbyterian & Reformed Publishing Company, 1961). What will surely become another classic book, critiquing the arguments of creationists through-out history, is Davis Young, *The Biblical Flood: A Case Study of the Church's Response to Extrabiblical Evidence* (Paternoster Press, 1995). Note also his earlier volume *Christianity and the Age of the Earth* (Zondervan, 1982).

Finally, a useful collection of essays about the patriarchs is A. R. Millard and D. J. Wiseman (eds.), *Essays on the Patriarchal Narratives* (IVP, 1980).

These books will give information about other books, enabling you to delve further. Some will be out of print, but you may be able to borrow them through your local library.